AN INTRODUCTION TO ENGLISH GRAMMAR

AN INTRODUCTION TO ENGLISH GRAMMAR

ADAM SPEERS

GYAN

Published by

GYAN

Gyan Publishing House
5, Ansari Road
Daryaganj, New Delhi-110002
Phone: 011-47034999, 9811692060
E-mail: books@gyanbooks.com

Distribution Network
gyanbooks.com
India, USA, Canada, UK, Australia

ISBN: 978-93-6780-348-6 (PB)

First Published, 1879

2nd Impression 2024

Printed at: Gyan Press, Delhi.

AN INTRODUCTION TO ENGLISH GRAMMAR

Author: ADAM SPEERS

AN INTRODUCTION

TO

ENGLISH GRAMMAR

INCLUDING THE

ANALYSIS OF SENTENCES:

WITH EXERCISES.

FOR THE USE OF SCHOOLS.

BY

ADAM SPEERS, B.Sc., LOND.,

HEAD-MASTER, THE SULLIVAN SCHOOLS, HOLYWOOD, BELFAST.

SECOND EDITION.

DUBLIN: SULLIVAN, BROTHERS,

LONDON: LONGMANS & CO.; SIMPKIN, MARSHALL, & CO.

MELBOURNE, SYDNEY, & ADELAIDE: G. ROBERTSON.

1880

PREFACE TO SECOND EDITION.

The favour with which this little work on English Grammar has been received by Educationists and the Press, encourages the Publishers to spare no pains to make the work a really valuable school-book. At the request of some eminent Teachers of English, a chapter on Punctuation has been added to this edition. Any further improvements recommended by Teachers will be respectfully considered.

Dublin, 1*st March*, 1880.

PREFACE.

In drawing up this little treatise, the Author has tried to present the principles of English Grammar in an intelligible and interesting form. The work embraces what he considers the *essentials* of the subject, and at the same time exhibits his views as to the manner in which the facts of Grammar should be brought before the minds of the young. The language used throughout being of the simplest possible kind, and the explanations and illustrations so full, it is hoped that, to pupils of ordinary capacity, the book will explain itself. As its title indicates, it is designed as an Introduction to the study of English. Prosody, Derivation, and Punctuation, are not dealt with at all; but the space thus saved has afforded the Author an opportunity of treating with greater fulness many important points which are either altogether omitted, or imperfectly explained, in most elementary Grammars.

Page 5 to page 39 is intended as a *first course* of English Grammar, which, it is believed, will be intelligible to any child capable of commencing the study of the subject; page 40 to page 93 may be made to form a *second course;* page 94 to the end will be found to furnish an amount of information on Syntax, Analysis, &c., quite sufficient for the requirements of the highest classes taught in ordinary schools.

The book contains a series of Exercises, which are neither too hard nor too numerous. These, it is hoped, will encourage the pupil to make a practical application of his knowledge of the text.

The Sullivan Schools, Holywood,
1st February, 1879.

CONTENTS.

ENGLISH GRAMMAR.

INTRODUCTION.

1. **Language** consists mainly of **Words**, and is the means which people employ to convey their thoughts to one another.

2. Words are spoken sounds, each of which denotes some idea. The sound of a word may be expressed by written characters, and so language may be either **spoken** or **written**.

3. Different nations make use of *different sets* of words. The collection of words used by any particular nation is the **Language** of that nation.

4. The **English Language** consists of the words in use among the British people. There are a great many thousands of them, as you may see by looking through a good English Dictionary.

5. Although words *separately* denote ideas, it is only when they are joined together in *groups* that they can express our thoughts. A group of words conveying a *complete sense* or *meaning* is called a **Sentence**. In conversation you are constantly using such groups, and your reading-books are full of them, every full stop bringing you to the end of one.

6. Sentences are of three kinds :—

(*a*) **Statements** ; as, "The fox is an animal of the dog kind." "No animals are commoner than spiders." "Birds fly and fishes swim."

(*b*) **Questions**; as, "Can a whelp bark?" "How many pupils are at school to-day?" "What is the use of a pen?"

(*c*) **Commands**, or **Entreaties**; as, "Tell me your name." "Answer me this question." "Forgive us our debts."

Notice that this mark (?), called a *Note of Interrogation*, is put after a question.

Exercise 1.

Distinguish orally or in writing the **Statements**, **Questions**, and **Commands** in the following sentences:—

Stand up. The farmer ploughs and sows. Is the corn ripe? The fox lapped it up very quickly. Bring me some ink. Did the lady call? Your writing is good. Show me your slate. Have you your lessons prepared? The tiger is an animal of the cat kind. Is the fire kindled? Ill weeds grow fast. Leave your jest when it's at the best. Stay at home. Will you be in town to-morrow? Cows and horses are useful animals. Do geese eat grass? Ducks swim and herons wade. Be gentle. Remember that one ought to do one's duty. Please excuse my delay. Could you work a sum in Proportion? I could. Why are you sad? Pardon me.

GRAMMAR AND SOME OF ITS DIVISIONS.

7. Grammar is the science of language in general, but **English grammar** deals only with the words which make up the English tongue.

8. English grammar treats of—

(*a*) The alphabet, spelling, &c.,	**Orthography.**
(*b*) The classification of words according to their uses in the sentence, (*c*) Inflection, or the changes in form (spelling), which some kinds of words undergo when we vary their application, (*d*) The derivation of words,	**Etymology.**
(*e*) How words are put together in a sentence, and how the words in a sentence are related to each other, (*f*) How sentences are related to each other,	**Syntax.**
(*g*) The laws of Poetry, Accent, &c.,	**Prosody.**

ORTHOGRAPHY.

9. Orthography treats of the letters of the **Alphabet** and **Spelling**.

10. All English words are formed from twenty-six letters, whose shapes and sounds you are supposed to be familiar with. They are called the **Alphabet**, or A B C, and are divided into two classes called **Vowels** and **Consonants**.

11. **Vowels*** are sounding letters—that is, they can be sounded continuously with the voice like a note in music. They are **a**, **e**, **i**, **o**, **u**, and sometimes **w** and **y**.

12. **W** is a vowel when it is united in sound with another vowel going before, as in *cow, flow*. **Y** is a vowel when it has the sound of "*i*," as in *Tyne, thyme, syrup*.

Notice that *w*=*u* in *cow*, which would be pronounced quite the same if spelt *cou*.

13. Two vowels blended into *one sound* form a **Diphthong**; as, *ou* in *sound*, *au* in *fraud*, *ow* in *cow*, *eu* in *feud*, *oa* in *broad*.

14. When *both* vowels are sounded, the diphthong is called **Proper**, as *ou* in *sound*; but when only *one* of the vowels is sounded, as *oa* in *cloak*, it is called **Improper**.

15. Three vowels blended into one sound form a **Triphthong**; as, *iew* in *view*, *ieu* in *adieu*.

16. **Consonants** are letters which cannot be perfectly sounded unless when put *before* or *after* the vowels; hence the name *consonant*, which means *sounding together with* (Lat. *consonans* = sounding together with).

17. Pronounce *go* and *og*. Now try to sound **g** without the vowel. You cannot do it except it be *before* it, as in *go*; or *after* it, as in *og*. This illustrates the nature of a consonant. But you must not confound the sound of a consonant with the *name* by which it is known; for example, *jee* is the name of the consonant

---

* Lat. *vocalis* = sounding. Fr. *voyelle*.

g; but *jee* is not its sound, as you may see by pronouncing *go*, *og*, *gog*, *gentle*.

18. The letters **w** and **y** are consonants when they come before a vowel in the same syllable, as in *wan*, *yelp*. It should also be mentioned that the letter **u** is a consonant when it follows **q**, as in *quite*, *queer*, *queen*.

Notice *queer* = *kweer*, *queen* = *kween*.

19. The sounds of the consonants are produced by means of the lips, teeth, throat, &c., which are called the organs of speech.

Lip-sounds, as *b*, *p*, *v*, are called **labials**.
Teeth-sounds, as *d*, *t*, *th*, are called **dentals**.
Throat-sounds, as *k*, *g* (hard), are called **gutturals**.
Nose-sounds, as *n*, *m*, *ng*, are called **nasals**.
Palate-sounds, as *j*, *g* (soft), are called **palatals**.
Hissing letters, as *s*, *z*, *x*, are called **sibilants**.

20. Consonants are divided into **mutes** or **dumb letters**, and **spirants**. In sounding a mute the breath is completely stopped; as, *c* (hard), *b*, *p*, *t*, in *cab*, *tap*, *cat*, *pact*. In sounding a spirant the breath is not quite shut off; as, *v*, *r*, *z*, *th*, in *vow*, *war*, *zeal*, *thin*.

21. The consonants, *l*, *m*, *n*, *r*, are called **liquids**, from the facility with which their sounds blend with those of other consonants. Observe this in the following words:—*help*, *hemp*, *pant*, *part*, *helmsman*, *ward*, *warn*, *armless*, *complete*.

Exercise 2.

Tell the Vowels, Consonants, Diphthongs, and Triphthongs in the following words:—

Beautiful, physics, aquatic, rowing, wonder, yonder, syllable, surrounded, conveyance, whoever, zoology, queer, viewing, universe.

SYLLABLES.

22. Letters are formed into **Syllables**; as, *dog*, *cat*, *mouse*. A syllable is pronounced by one effort of the organs of speech.

23. A syllable must contain at least one vowel, and may even be a single vowel; as, *o-ver*, in which the first syllable is the vowel "o," and the second, "*ver*," contains one, viz., e.

24. Syllables form words. A word is called a **Monosyllable** if it contains only *one* syllable; as, *man*; a **Dissyllable** if it contains *two*; as, *man-kind*; a **Trisyllable** if it contains *three*; as, *re-pre-sent*; and a **Polysyllable** if it contains *four* or more; as, *re-pre-sen-ta-tive.*

25. To **spell** a word is to name in order the *letters* of which it is made up, and mark its *syllables*, should it contain two or more. Thus in spelling the word "*composition*," you should say COM-PO-SI-TION, making a short pause after each syllable.

26. **Learn the following rules for dividing words:—**

(*a*) Never divide a monosyllable; as, *house, field.*

(*b*) Separate two consonants coming together; as, *m* and *p* in *temper*, thus—*tem-per*; but don't separate *b* and *l* in *able*, *t* and *h* in *heather*, for that would destroy the proper sounds of the words.

(*c*) Separate two vowels not forming a diphthong; as, *e* and *a* in *meander*; also a vowel and a diphthong; as, *oy* and *i* in *boy-ish.*

(*d*) Endings such as *ing*, *ed*, *ance*, *tion*, &c., should be separated; as, call-*ing*, lov-*ed*, as-sist-*ance*, na-*tion.*

(*e*) Be guided by the separate efforts required to pronounce words slowly and correctly.

Exercise 3.

(*a*.) Divide *orally* or in *writing* the following words into Syllables:—

Character, polysyllable, parallel, excellent, feebleness, antecedent, house, diphthong, melancholy, incomprehensibility, authoritative, over, any, zoology, blind, untrodden, classification, man, special, substantial, undoubtedly, doubt.

(*b*.) Write six Monosyllables, six Dissyllables, six Trisyllables, and six Polysyllables.

Caution.—When writing, if you have not sufficient room for a word of two or more syllables at the end of a line, stop at the end

of a syllable, make this mark (—), and write the rest of the word at the beginning of the next line. Recollect you must not divide a monosyllable.

CAPITAL AND SMALL LETTERS.

27. The alphabet is written and printed in several ways; but the most important forms are **Capitals**, as, A, B, C; **Small letters**, as, a, b, c; and **Italics**, as, *a, b, c.* The small letters are most used; but putting a *capital* where a *small letter* ought to be, or a small letter for a capital, is regarded as an error in spelling and a sign of ignorance.

28. The following simple rules will guide you in using capital letters.

Capital letters should be used at the beginning of—

(*a*) The **first word** of a **sentence** and the **first word of a line in poetry**; as, "My friends are kind." "Where is France situated?"

"Till last by Philip's farm I flow
To join the brimming river;
For men may come and men may go,
But I go on for ever."

(*b*) The **names and titles of Deity**; as, *God, Jehovah, The Almighty;* also the words "He," "Thou," &c., when applied to Deity.

(*c*) The **names of individuals**; as, *John, Mary, England, Ireland;* and such words as, *English, Irish.*

(*d*) The **names of the months**; as, *January;* and the days of the week; as, *Friday.*

(*e*) The **first word of a quotation**; as, Solomon says, "All is vanity."

(*f*) **Any important word**; as, the *Crusades;* also I and O when used as words.

Exercise 4.

Correct in writing the *misplaced Capitals* and *Small letters* in the following sentences:—

milton was a great Poet. **spain and Portugal form a Peninsula *in the South-west of* europe. god made everything, and we Know**

that he Sustains all Things that live. Shakespeare says, "to be or not to be, that is the Question."

> **"come back ! Come back !" he cried in grief,**
> **across this Stormy Water,**
> **and i'll forgive your Highland chief,**
> **My Daughter, o my Daughter !"**

The last month of the Year is december. Monday is the Second and saturday is the Seventh day of the Week.

ETYMOLOGY.

29. Etymology treats of—

(*a*) The **classification of words** ;
(*b*) The **inflection of words** ;
(*c*) The **derivation of words.**

THE CLASSIFICATION OF WORDS.

30. Words are put into different classes according to the different uses they serve in a sentence. For example, some words are used as *names* of objects ; others, *to state ;* others, *to describe* things ; others, to make *connections* and denote *relations.*

31. There are eight classes of words commonly known as the eight **Parts of Speech** :—

The **Noun.**	The **Adverb.**
The **Adjective.**	The **Preposition.**
The **Pronoun.**	The **Conjunction.**
The **Verb.**	The **Interjection.**

DEFINITIONS OF THE PARTS OF SPEECH.

32. When a word is used as a *name* of any kind it is called a **Noun** ; as, *James, Dublin, horse, health, thunder.*

33. Adjectives are words put along with Nouns for the purpose of *describing* or *distinguishing* them in any way ; as, "*A certain* man had *the good* luck to possess *a valuable* goose that laid *one golden* egg *every* day." *A, certain, the, good, valuable, one, golden,* and *every* are *Adjectives.*

NOTE.—The Adjectives *a*, *an*, and *the* are often called Articles.

34. A **Pronoun** is a word that *stands for* a Noun; as, "When William found the book *which* Jane had lost *he* restored *it* to *her*." *Which*, *he*, *it*, and *her* are Pronouns.

35. A **Verb** *states*, *commands*, or *asks*, but its chief use is to state; as, "The sun *shines*," "*Stand* up," "*Is* John at school?" *Shines*, *stand*, and *is* are Verbs.

36. An **Adverb** is a word that modifies the meaning of a Verb, an Adjective, or another Adverb; as, "He acted *wisely*," "The sun is *very* bright," "He ran *too fast*." *Wisely*, *very*, *too*, and *fast* are Adverbs.

37. **Prepositions** are words placed before Nouns or Pronouns *to connect them with* and *show their relation to* Verbs, Adjectives, or other Nouns or Pronouns; as, "An owl, anxious *for* supper, sat *upon* a wall *behind* an old ruin, *with* the intention *of* pouncing *on* any mouse or little bird that might come *near* it." *For*, *upon*, *behind*, *with*, *of*, *on*, and *near* are Prepositions.

38. **Conjunctions** join together *sentences* and *words*, but their chief use is to connect sentences; as "Birds fly *and* fishes swim," "*Neither* James *nor* William came," "My brother is come, *but* I have not seen him." *And*, *neither*, *nor*, and *but*, are Conjunctions.

39 **Interjections** are exclamations thrown in among other words to call attention; as, *Ho!* or to express some strong sudden feeling; as, *Ah! Oh! Alas! Hurrah!*

THE NOUN.*

40. When a word is used as a *name* of any kind, it is called a **Noun.**

NOTE.—The word *noun* means a *name*.

Names of **persons** are Nouns; as, *Adam*, *Anne*;
Names of **animals** are Nouns; as, *cow*, *sheep*;

---

* Lat. *nomen* = a name.

Names of **places** are Nouns ; as, *Ireland, London ;*
Names of **material things** are Nouns ; as, *gold, silver ;*
Names of **feelings** are Nouns ; as, *pain, hunger ;*
Names of **qualities** are Nouns ; as, *weight, brightness ;* and,
Names of **actions** are also Nouns ; as, "*Walking* and *riding* are healthful exercises." *Walking* and *riding* here name two actions, therefore they are Nouns.

41. The *names* of things are Nouns, but not the *things* themselves. For example, your *name* is a Noun, but *you* are not a Noun ; and, in like manner, the word *ship* is a Noun, but the *thing* ship is *not*.

THE DIFFERENT KINDS OF NOUNS.

42. Nouns are divided into three great classes :—

1. **Proper Nouns.**
2. **Common Nouns.**
3. **Abstract Nouns.**

43. A **Proper Noun** is the name of *one* person, *one* place, or *one* thing in the same sense ; as *Richard, Mary, Dublin, Bounce, Excalibur.*

44. The word *proper* is derived from the Latin *proprius* = "one's own ;" a proper name therefore means *one's own* name, or the name specially belonging to an individual of any kind. Thus—

Richard is the name of an *individual* boy.
Mary is the name of an *individual* girl.
Dublin is the name of an *individual* town.
Bounce is the name of an *individual* dog.
Excalibur was the name of King Arthur's sword.

Note.—When writing a Proper Noun, begin with a capital letter.

45. A **Common Noun** is a name *common* to each individual in the same class or kind of things ; as, boy, girl, *pupil, house.*

Notice that the name *boy* is common to every male pupil in the school; that is, any one of them may be called a boy; as, *John* is a boy, *James* is a boy, &c. Similarly the name *girl* may be applied to *Jane*, *Mary*, *Rachel*, &c.; and you may call every boy and girl in the school a *pupil*. The word *house* may, in the same way, be applied to *any* house in the town. This explains why such names as *boy*, *girl*, *pupil*, *house*, are called *Common* Nouns.

46. Common nouns include **Collective Nouns**. A **Collective Noun** stands for a *collection* of persons or things considered as *one*; as, *the Parliament*, *the army*, *a jury*, *a group*, *a gang*, *a mob*, *a lot*. Notice that "the Parliament" denotes *one body* made up of *separate* individuals—the Members; and "the army" denotes *one body* made up of *separate* individuals—the soldiers.

Exercise 5.

Pick out the **Proper**, **Common**, and **Collective** Nouns in the following:—

The cherry-tree is a native of Asia, and was first brought to Europe by Lucullus.

The leaves of the black currant have a strong taste, and if a portion be mixed with black tea, the flavour will become like that of green tea. Currant bushes are an ornament to a garden; and when they are trained against the walls of a cottage, they look like the vines of Italy and Spain.

A collection of words conveying a sense or meaning is called a sentence. There was a multitude of men present. A constellation is a group of fixed stars. The Parliament is sitting. The Speaker presides over the House. The Committee appointed John to take charge of the school. There was a party at the Castle last night. The army is well trained.

Abstract Nouns.

47. **Abstract Nouns are names of**—

(*a*) **Qualities**; as, *whiteness*, *colour*, *weight*.
(*b*) **States** or **conditions**; as, *hunger*, *thirst*, *death*.
(*c*) **Actions**; as, *march*, *move*, *flight*, *step*.

48. *Abstract* Nouns may be formed from Adjectives

of Quality (See § 56) by adding *ness*, *ty*, *ice*, *th*, &c.; as—

ADJECTIVE.		ABSTRACT NOUN.	ADJECTIVE.		ABSTRACT NOUN.
Good	becomes	*goodness.*	*Strong*	becomes	*strength.*
Just	„	*justice.*	*Broad*	„	*breadth.*
Pure	„	*purity.*	*White*	„	*whiteness.*

Adjectives of Quality also become Abstract Nouns when they stand alone with *the* or a *Preposition* before them; as, "the *grand*," "the *tender*," "the *severe*." "The music changed from *solemn* to *lively*." *Grand*, *tender*, *severe*, *solemn*, and *lively* are Abstract Nouns.

49. Read the following sentences:—

"John is making a *move* on the chess-board."
"I hear the *march* of armed men."
"His *step* is firm."

Here *move*, *march*, and *step* are Abstract Nouns, being the names of actions. But when I say: "*Move* on;" "He *shall march*;" "*Step* over the stile;" *move*, *march*, and *step* are Verbs. You must not parse any word as a Noun unless it be **really used as a name**; thus, *John* is a Verb and not a Noun in the sentence, "Don't *John* me so much."

Exercise 6.

(a.) Tell the **Abstract Nouns** in the following:—

"That very queer sound,—
Does it come from the ground?
It is not like talking, it is not like walking,
It's not like the clattering of pot or of pan,
Or the tramp of a horse, or the tread of a man,
Or the hum of a crowd, or the shouting of boys,
It's really a very odd sort of a noise!"

The brightness of the sun is great. Cherish a sense of honour. John's health is impaired. The whiteness and purity of snow are remarkable. There is a land where parting is unknown.

"Beyond the flight of time,
Beyond this vale of death,
There surely is some blessed clime
Where life is not a breath,
Nor life's affections transient fire,
Whose sparks fly upwards and expire."

(*b*.) Give orally or in writing **Abstract Nouns** from the following words :—

Hard, narrow, wide, deep, true, false, severe, easy, difficult, kind, kindly, king.

THE ADJECTIVE.*

50. Adjectives are words put along with Nouns for the purpose of describing or distinguishing them in any way; as, "*A certain* man had *the good* luck to possess *a valuable* goose which laid *one golden* egg *every* day."

The Adjectives in this sentence are—*a*, *certain*, *the*, *good*, *valuable*, *one*, *golden*, *every*. Notice that the two Adjectives *a* and *certain* are added to the Noun *man* to show that *one* man owned the goose, but that I either *cannot* or *do not choose* to name him (*a certain* man); *the* points out the Noun *luck*, and *good* shows its *kind* (*the good* luck); *a* goose means *one* goose, and *valuable* tells the *kind* of goose (*a valuable* goose); *one* shows *how many* eggs the goose laid in a day, and *golden* tells the *kind* of egg (*one golden* egg); and *every* shows on *how many* days in succession the goose laid (*every* day).

Strictly speaking the Adjective does not describe or distinguish the *Noun*, but the *thing* or *things* which the Noun *denotes*.

51. Adjectives are divided according to their uses into the following kinds :—

1. **Demonstrative Adjectives.**
2. **Adjectives of Number and Quantity.**
3. **Adjectives of Quality.**
4. **Adjectives denoting Possession.**

52. Demonstrative Adjectives *point out* the Nouns to which they belong. They all answer the question "**Which?**" addressed to the Noun; as, "Which pen?" *Ans.* "*The* pen, *this* pen, *yon* pen, *that* pen, the *first* pen, the *second* pen."

53. The words **a**, **an**, and **the**, are often called **Articles**. *The* is called the **Definite**, and *a* or *an* the **Indefinite Article**.

---

* Lat. *adjectus* = added to.

An is used before a *vowel* or a silent *h*, as, "*an* egg," "*an* honest man;" **a** is put before a consonant; as, "*a* pen," "*a* slate."

A may be put before a word beginning with an *aspirated* vowel, that is, a vowel pronounced as if it were preceded by **y** or **w**; as, a *ew*er, a *u*nit, a *o*ne pound note.

Notice that *ew*er=*yew*er, *u*nit=*yu*nit, *o*ne=*wo*n.

54. The *points out clearly* a particular thing, or particular things, of the kind or class which the Noun denotes; **a** indicates *one* of the kind or class which the Noun denotes, but does not point out *which* one. Thus when I say "Lend me *the* pen," "*the* pen" is equivalent to *you know which* pen; but when I say "Lend me *a* pen," *a* pen is equivalent to *one* pen, but I don't say *which*. **The** is, therefore, a **Demonstrative** Adjective; and **a** or **an**, an Adjective of **Number**.

55. Adjectives denoting **Number** answer the question, "**How many?**" addressed to the Noun; as, "How many men?" Ans. *Two* men, *twenty* men, *few* men, *many* men, *no* men. **Indefinite** Numeral Adjectives are such as do not denote an exact number; as, *few*, *many*, *several*, *some*, &c.

When Adjectives express **Quantity**, they answer the question, "**How much?**" as, "How much pain?" Ans. *Great* pain, *little* pain, *much* pain, *more* pain, *no* pain.

56. Adjectives of **Quality** answer the question, "**What sort?**" addressed to the Noun; as, "What sort of a man?" Ans. A *good* man, a *bad* man, a *rich* man, a *poor* man, an *honest* man, a *learned* man, an *ignorant* man, an *intelligent* man. This is the largest class of Adjectives.

You will notice that it is from this class chiefly that Abstract Nouns are formed.

57. Adjectives denoting **Possession** answer the question, "**Whose?**" addressed to the Noun; as, "Whose book?" Ans. *My* book, *your* book, *his own* book, *their own* books.

The Possessive Adjectives are **my**, **thy**, **his**, **her**, **its**, *our*, *your*. **their**, and **own**, which may be put after each of the eight others to express possession with more emphasis; as, "*my own* house," which is more emphatic than "*my* house." **My, thy,** &c., are simply Pronouns used as Adjectives, and may be parsed as such. See § 156.

58. A Possessive Adjective is always followed in the sentence by a Noun denoting the thing possessed; as, my *books*, his *books*, your *books*, their *books*.

Mine and **thine** are sometimes put before Nouns beginning with a vowel, and are then Possessive Adjectives; as, "Pardon *mine* iniquities;" "If *thine* eye offend thee, pluck it out."

59. Notice that when I say, "The pen is mine," "*mine*" is not followed by a Noun, and is equivalent to *my pen*. *Mine* thus *stands for* the Noun "*pen*," as well as for the *name* of the *possessor* of the pen, and should be parsed as a **Possessive Pronoun.** Parse, in like manner, *yours*, *theirs*, as Possessive Pronouns in "The books are *yours*," "The books are *theirs*." See § 157.

60. Nouns may be used as Adjectives; as, "a *gold* watch," "a *brass* button." Adjectives are often used as Nouns; as, "John is going from *bad* to *worse*," "the *beautiful*," "the *awful*."

61. Some **kinds** of Adjectives are found as often *after* as *before* the Nouns to which they belong; as, "Frank is *truthful*." Observe that when an Adjective is thus used (as a predicate), it may qualify a **Pronoun** or any **group of words** equivalent to a Noun; as, "He is *diligent*;" "To be truthful is *honourable*." Parse *diligent* an Adjective qualifying *he*, and *honourable* an Adjective qualifying "*to be truthful*." See p. 104.

Exercise 7.

Point out *orally* or in *writing* the different kinds of Adjectives in the following, and tell the Nouns to which they belong.

Remember that Demonstrative Adjectives answer the question "Which?" addressed to the Noun; Adjectives of Number and Quantity, the question "How many?" or "How much?"; Adjectives of Quality, the question "What kind?"; and Adjectives denoting Possession, the question "Whose?" Find in this way the different kinds of Adjectives.

The camel is from five to seven feet high, and his length is about ten feet. His legs are long, his neck is long and crooked, and his head is small. There are two species of camel; one has two humps, and the other only one. The latter kind is somewhat smaller than the former, but in other respects the one differs little from the other. The camel is covered with coarse hair; his colour is light brown, and his feet are soft and flat like large pads. The camel is of much use in countries where there is little water.

Sunday is the first and Saturday the last day of the week. Twelve articles make one dozen. Sixty seconds make one minute. The first and last duty of a soldier is obedience. James has no bad marks.

THE PRONOUN.

62. A **Pronoun** is a word that stands for a Noun; as, "When William found the book *which* Jane had lost, *he* restored *it* to *her*."

The little words, "which," "he," "it," and "her," are Pronouns, each standing for a Noun: viz., which, for *book*; he, for *William*; it, for *book*; and her, for *Jane*.

The word *pronoun* means "*for* a noun," being derived from Lat. *pro* = for, and *noun*.

63. Pronouns prevent the necessity of having to repeat the Nouns too often. For example, if we had no Pronouns, instead of saying, "When William found the book which Jane had lost, he restored it to her;" we should have to say, "William found the book," "Jane had lost the book," "William restored the book to Jane."

CLASSIFICATION OF PRONOUNS.

64. Pronouns are divided into the following kinds :—

1. Personal Pronouns.
2. Relative Pronouns.
3. Demonstrative Pronouns.
4. Interrogative Pronouns.
5. Indefinite Pronouns.

65. **Personal Pronouns** are simple substitutes for *the names of* persons, places, and things. They are—I,

thou, he, she, it, one; with their variations—**mine, me, him, her, we, you, they, them**, &c. These Pronouns are called *Personal*, because they denote—

(*a*) The **person speaking**; as, *I, mine, me.*
(*b*) The **person spoken to**; as, *thou, thine, thee.*
(*c*) The **person spoken of**; as, *he, she, her.*

66. When a Personal Pronoun denotes the **speaker**, it is said to be of the **First Person**; as, "Give that to *me*" = Give that to me (the speaker). When a Personal Pronoun denotes a **person addressed**, it is of the **Second Person**; as, "Do you (the person addressed) hear me?" When a Personal Pronoun denotes a **person** or **thing spoken of**, it is of the **Third Person**; as, "*He* (the person spoken of) told me."

67. *Myself, thyself, yourself, himself, itself, ourselves, yourselves, themselves*, are **Compound Personal Pronouns**; and in such expressions as, "He warmed *himself*," "I hurt *myself*," &c., they are named **Reflexive Pronouns.**

Exercise 8.

Write out the following narrative, and put Nouns in place of the Pronouns, which are italicised.

A lark having built *her* nest in a field of corn, *it* grew ripe before *her* young ones were able to fly. Fearing lest *they* should be destroyed when the corn would be reaping, *she* told *them* before *she* went out to get *them* food, that *they* must listen if *they* should hear anything said about reaping *it*. At *her* return *they* told *her* that the farmer and *his* son had been there, and had agreed to ask *their* neighbours to assist *them* in cutting *it*. "Then *I* may let *you* remain another day," said *she* to *them*.

RELATIVE PRONOUNS.

68. Relative Pronouns are so called because they **relate** or **carry us back** to an *antecedent* Noun or Pronoun in the sentence; as,

"I received the *present* (*Ant.*) *which* (*Rel.*) you sent me."

"*He* (*Ant.*) prayeth best *who* (*Rel.*) loveth most."

Observe the connection between the Relative Pronoun *and its Antecedent.*

69. The Relative may have **a sentence** for its **Antecedent**; as, "*The weather is fine*, *which* makes it very pleasant."
Ant. *Rel.*

70. The Relative Pronouns are **who, which, that, what, whom, whose,** and **as**, called **Simple Relatives**; and **whoever, whichever, whatever, whosoever, whichsoever,** and **whatsoever**, named **Compound Relatives**.

71. **What** means "*that which*;" as, "Do *what* I desire you" = "Do *that which* I desire you."

72. **Who** stands for *persons*, **which** for *animals* and *lifeless things*, **that** may take the place of either *who* or *which*, and thus prevent the too frequent repetition of either. Thus we can say, "the man *who* came," or "the man *that* came," but not "the man *which* came; "the stars *that* twinkle," or "the stars *which* twinkle," but not "the stars *who* twinkle;" "the dog *which* or the dog *that* barks," but not "the dog *who* barks."

73. Relative Pronouns not only **take the place of Nouns**, but also **join one sentence to another**. Thus, in the sentence, "I have seen the house *which* you built," "*which*," the relative, **connects** "*I have seen the house*" with "*you built*," and, at the same time, **stands instead of** "house."

NOTE.—Relatives might be called Conjunctive Pronouns.

74. Call **as** a Relative after *same, such*, as *much*, as *many*; as, "Yours are the same *as* mine;" "Such *as* come are welcome."

DEMONSTRATIVE PRONOUNS.

75. DEMONSTRATIVE PRONOUNS stand for Nouns, and **define** them; as, "*This* is better than *that*." Parse *this* and *that* in the above sentence as Demonstrative Pronouns; and note that if the sentence were, "*This* thing is better than *that* thing," you should parse *this* and *that* Demonstrative Adjectives.

76. The Demonstrative Pronouns are **this, that, these, those, you, such, the same.** They can all be used as *Adjectives*.

77. *This* and *these* refer to things near; *that*, *those*, and *yon* to things more distant. *This* and *these* also point out the *last* named, and *that* and *those* the *first* named, of two things mentioned in connection with each other; as,

> "Farewell, my friends; farewell, my foes!
> My peace with *these*, my love with *those*."

These = "my foes;" *those* = "my friends."

INTERROGATIVE PRONOUNS.

78. INTERROGATIVE PRONOUNS **ask questions.** They are **who? which?** and **what?**

79. *Who* asks a person's **name**; as, "*Who* is that?" Ans. "*John*." *Which* may refer to either **persons** or **things**; as, "*Which* is the *way*?" "*Which* of *you* did it?" *What*, as an Interrogative Pronoun, refers to **things only**; as, "*What* is that?"="What *thing* is that?"

80. *Which* and *what* are often **Interrogative Adjectives**; as, "*Which* girl?" "*What* boy?" Notice that, as an Adjective, *what* may refer to persons.

INDEFINITE PRONOUNS.

81. INDEFINITE PRONOUNS stand for Nouns, but **do not point them out clearly.** They are **any, all, few, some, several, one, other, another, none, each, every, either, neither, nobody, somebody, anybody, something, nothing, aught, naught,** &c.

82. Most of the Indefinite Pronouns may be used as Adjectives. Parse them as Adjectives when they are *put before* Nouns, and as Pronouns when they *take the place* of Nouns. In the following sentence, "*Some* like study, *others* like play," "*some*" and "*others*" are Indefinite Pronouns; but in "*Some* boys like study, *other* boys like play," "*some*" and "*other*" are Indefinite Adjectives.

NOTE.—*Each other* and *one another* are called **Reciprocal Pronouns.**

83. Learn from the following examples the differ-

ence between Indefinite Pronouns and Indefinite Adjectives :—

Sentences containing Indefinite Pronouns.	**Sentences containing Indefinite Adjectives.**
Several were present.	*All* men are mortal.
One consents, *another* refuses.	*Every* boy should go out in his order.
The laws are made for *all* and *sundry.*	*Several* persons came.
Has *anybody aught* against him?	I was there the *other* day.
Somebody must be head of the class.	*Either* ball will do.
Some were saved.	I met James *one* day in town.
Each got a prize.	Did you catch *any* fish to-day?
	Each girl got a prize.

Exercise 9.

(*a.*) Pick out and classify the **Pronouns** which occur in the following sentences :—

That is work of waste and ruin : do as Charles and I are doing. Who killed Cock Robin? "I," said the sparrow. Tom's horse is larger than that of his brother. Who are you? Did anybody see him? This is what I want. Any may come, none are excluded. Nobody came. One ought to know one's own mind. The book which he found is mine. Are these marbles yours? Bring the map that you were sent for. Tell me the name of those that make cloth. She is one that everybody respects. What is that?

(*b.*) Supply the **Relatives** which are omitted.

That is the teacher —— taught me, and there is the school—— I attended. I have got —— I wanted. The friend —— helps in need is a true friend. John —— was present heard everything —— was said. Wellington was a general of —— all Englishmen are proud. Frank has a dog —— barks. I give you such —— I have. He —— we worship, by —— gift we live, and by —— all things were made is the Lord.

(*c.*) Supply **Antecedents.** Did you like the —— which he sang? John has a —— that mews, and a —— that sings. James has a —— that trots fast. The —— which you read is interesting. Give the —— that you have for saying so. Did you get the —— which he sent you? This is the —— that killed the rat. —— whom we worship, made all —— that exist. —— who lies, would steal.

(*d.*) Correct the following :—Return the book whom I gave you. This is the cat who killed the rat. Beware the train who is coming. John is a boy which I believe. The bird whom I caught flew away. John has a watch who keeps good time. Frank is a boy which I like. I lost my pencil ; but Jane found her. Men should not spend his time foolishly.

THE VERB.*

84. A **Verb states, commands**, or **asks**; but its *chief use* is to state.

85. A Verb **states**:—

(*a*) What anything **does**; as,

"Dogs *bark*." "Ships *sail*." "The wind *blows*."

(*b*) What **is done to** anything; as,

"The bird *was shot*." "John *was struck*.

(*c*) What anything **is**, or what **is the condition** of anything; as,

"The moon *is* round." "John *is sleeping*."

Verbs **command**; as,

"*Come* back." "*Stand* there." "*March*."

Verbs **ask questions**; as,

"*Are* the apples ripe?" "*Do* hawks *kill* little birds?"

Note.—Without a Verb you could not make a statement. It is the essential part of speech in every sentence; hence the name "*verb*" which means the word.

86. A Verb may be a **single word**; as, "fishes *swim*;" or it may consist of **two, three**, or **four words**; as, "Samuel *can write*" (two words); "The task *should be learned*" (three words); "The copy *should have been written*" (four words).

Observe that it takes the two words, "*can write*," to state what Samuel **can do**; the three words, "*should be learned*," to state what **should be done to** the task; and the four words, "*should have been written*," to state what **should have been done to** the copy.

SUBJECT AND DIRECT OBJECT.

87. When a Verb is used for stating or asserting there must be *something* about which the assertion is made. This is called the **SUBJECT** of the Verb; and also

* **Lat. *verbum*=the word.**

the Subject of the sentence. It may be found by putting the question, "WHO?" or "WHAT?" before the Verb.

Examine these sentences—

"He fell."
"Charles was beheaded."
"To be truthful is honourable."

Now ask, "Who or what fell?" "Who or what was beheaded?" "Who or what is honourable?" and you get the answers—"*he*," "*Charles*," and "*to be truthful*."

"**He**" is the Subject of the Verb "*fell*,"
"**Charles**" is the Subject of the Verb "*was beheaded*,"
"**To be truthful**" is the Subject of the Verb "*is*."

The Subject of a Verb is often called the **Nominative Case** to the Verb. Know it by both names, and remember that it is always a **Noun** or a **Pronoun**, or a **group of words** equivalent to a Noun.

88. Read and examine carefully these two sentences—

1. "The river runs."
2. "**The smith shod the horse.**"

The Verb "*runs*" here states what its Subject (*river*) **does**; viz., "The river **runs**;" and the sense is perfect. You don't think of asking, "The river runs (what?);" for the action of running is not **done to** anything. In the second sentence it is quite different. The Verb "*shod*" **states** what its Subject (the *smith*) **did**; **viz.**, the **smith shod**; but the sense is *not* perfect until you **know** what the shoeing **was done to**, which you may learn by putting (WHAT?) after "*shod*," thus, "The smith shod (what?)" **Ans.** "The horse." "*Horse*" is necessary to complete the sense, and is called the **DIRECT OBJECT** of the verb "*shod*." The Direct Object is often called the **Objective Case** governed by the Verb. Know it by both names; and remember that it is always a **Noun**, or a **Pronoun**, or a **group of words** equivalent to a Noun.

CLASSIFICATION OF VERBS.

89. Verbs are divided according to their nature and meaning into two **great classes**:—

1. **Transitive** Verbs.
2. **Intransitive** Verbs.

90. The action of a Transitive Verb **is done to something**; as, "The smith shod the *horse*," "*Charles* was beheaded." The action of shoeing was done to the horse, and the action of beheading was done to Charles; therefore, "*shod*" and "*was beheaded*" are **Transitive** Verbs. What the action of a Transitive Verb is *done to*, is called **the Object of the Action.** "*Horse*" is the Object of the Action of the Verb "*shod*," and "*Charles*" is the Object of the Action of the Verb "*was beheaded.*" The *Object of the Action* is called the **Direct Object** when it follows the Verb thus: "The smith shod the horse" (see § 88);

Trans. Verb. (shod) — *Direct Obj.* (horse)

but it may also be used as the **Subject** of the Verb; *e.g.*, "The horse was shod by the smith," "*Charles* was beheaded."

Subject (horse) — *Trans. Verb.* (was shod)

91. The action expressed by an Intransitive Verb **is not done to** anything; as, "The child *is weeping*." "The wind *blows*."

"*Is weeping*" and "*blows*" are **Intransitive Verbs.**

92. Most Verbs imply **action**, but some—usually called **Neuter** Verbs—do not. Here are examples:—

"John *is* a good boy.
"The bill *remains* due."
"Smith *became* a good scholar."
"The weather *continues* fine."

MEANING OF ACTIVE VOICE AND PASSIVE VOICE.

93. Look at the following statement:—

"John found a purse."

Here "*John*" is the SUBJECT of the Verb "*found*," and "*purse*" is its Object; that is, "*purse*" is what the action *was done to*. But **John, the Subject**, is also the **doer** of the action, as you may see by asking, "Who did it?" or "Who found a purse?" **Ans.** "John." The Verb "*found*" *is, for* this reason, said to be in the **ACTIVE VOICE.**

Definition.—When the **Subject** of a Verb **does the action,** the Verb is said to be in the **ACTIVE VOICE.**

94. Look at this statement—

"A purse was found by John."

Here "*purse*" is the SUBJECT of the Verb "*was found,*" because it answers the question "What was found?" Ans. "A purse." It is also the OBJECT of the action expressed by the Verb; because the action *was done to the purse.* Thus "**purse,**" the subject, denotes the **Object or receiver** of the action, and "*was found*" is, for this reason, said to be in the **PASSIVE VOICE.**

Definition.—When the **action** expressed by a *Transitive* Verb **is done to the Subject,** the Verb is said to be **in the PASSIVE VOICE.**

95. The ACTIVE may be changed to the PASSIVE voice without altering the meaning of the sentence. Thus we can say—

Active Voice.	Passive Voice.
The master *taught* James.	James *was taught* by the master.
I *lost* a halfpenny.	A halfpenny *was lost* by me.
James *struck* Frank.	Frank *was struck* by James.
Jane *likes* Mary.	Mary *is liked* by Jane.
Tom *should learn* music.	Music *should be learned* by Tom.

96. Be sure that you thoroughly understand the following:—

(*a*) The **Object of the Action** of a Transitive Verb means simply the Noun, Pronoun, or equivalent of a Noun, which denotes what the action *is done to;* as, "*James* was struck." "John struck *James.*"

Object. Trans. Verb. — *Tr. Verb. Object.*

(*b*) When the Voice is **Active,** the *Object of the Action* is the **Direct Object** or *Objective Case governed by the Verb;* and the *doer* or *agent* of the action is the **Subject** or Nominative; as, "*John* struck *James.*"

Subject and Agent. — *Act. Voice.* — *Direct Obj.*

(*c*) **When the Voice is Passive,** the Object of the Action **becomes the Subject** of the Verb, and the agent, when expressed, is indicated by means of the Preposition "*by;*" as, "*James* was struck by *John.*"

Subject and Obj. of Act. — *Pass. Voice.* — *Agent.*

THE INFINITIVE.

97. That form of the Verb which takes the word "*to*" before it, is called the **Infinitive**; *e.g., to learn, to sing, to be praised, to be punished.* When a Verb takes this form it does not state, command, or ask; but either simply names or expresses in a general way, whatever idea the Verb implies; whether of "*doing,*" "*being done to,*" or "*being.*" The Infinitive thus partakes of the nature of a Noun, and is indeed sometimes the equivalent of one; *e.g.*:—

"*To learn* is profitable."
"Nobody likes *to be punished.*"

Here the Infinitives "*to learn*" and "*to be punished*" are equivalent to the Abstract Nouns "*learning*" and "*punishment.*" "*To learn*" is the Subject of the Verb "*is,*" and "*to be punished*" is the Direct Object of the Verb "*likes;*" thus:—

To learn (*Infinitive.*) is profitable = Learning (*Abstract Noun.*) is profitable.

Nobody likes to be punished (*Infinitive.*) = Nobody likes punishment (*Abstract Noun.*).

The word "*to*" belongs to the Verb, in such cases, and is not to be parsed as a Preposition; it is simply the sign of the Infinitive.

For further information on the Infinitive, see § 193 to § 195 inclusive.

PARTICIPLES.

98. The form of the Verb which ends in *ing* is called the **Present Participle**; as, *singing, working.* Another form which ends in *ed, d, t, en, n,* &c., is called the **Past Participle**; as, *loved, heard, meant, written, lain.* Participles in *ing* and the Past Participles of Transitive Verbs

may be used purely as **Adjectives**; as, a *singing* bird, a *wounded* soldier. Participles often form the **chief parts** of **stating Verbs**; as, "The bird *is singing*," "I *have written* a letter." You may find the Past Participle by trying **"I have"** before the Verb. Thus, you can say "I have *seen*," "I have *written*," but not "I have *saw*," "I have *wrote*;" *seen* and *written* are therefore Past Participle forms. The **Present** Participle may be used as a **Noun**; e.g., "*Seeing* is *believing*."

Participles *participate* in the nature of Verbs and Adjectives, or of Verbs and Nouns, hence their name.

For further information, see § 196 to § 202, inclusive.

Exercise 10.

(*a*.) Write out six **Assertions**, six **Questions**, and six **Commands**, using different Verbs.

(*b*.) Supply **omitted Subjects** in the following :—

—— is called the New World. —— have branches. —— is the capital of Ireland. —— roar. —— fly. —— conquered Napoleon. —— is an article of food. —— is commendable. —— swim.

Supply **Direct Objects** which are **omitted** :—

William tore ——. James took ——. Who killed ——? Jane sang ——. The mason built ——. He spent ——. He felled ——. Bob hurt ——. The master praised ——. The boy loves ——.

(*c*.) Change the following Verbs from the **Active Voice** to the **Passive Voice** without altering the sense :—

The sun gives light. Joiners make chairs. They weeded the field. The hound caught a hare. The maid has milked the cow. The sparrow killed cock-robin. James will build a house. The farmer had sown the seed. The farmer will have sown the seed by next May. John makes fair promises.

(*d*.) Change the following Verbs from the **Passive** to the **Active Voice** without altering the sense :—

The town is taken by the soldiers. Osman was wounded by a bullet. John has been praised by the master. William will be punished by his father. Paris was besieged by the Germans. The Livingstone River was traced by Stanley. Good boys are loved by their teachers. The window had been left open by the servant. Your time has been wasted. Frank might have been killed by the horse.

(*c.*) **Tell the Infinitive**, the **Present Participle**, and the **Past Participle** of the Verbs which occur in the following :—

The tree fell. The canary flew away. James won the game. The door is shut. The gun burst. Frank worked his sum. Come nearer me. I hear the music. Do you like music? The grass has been mown. John spilled the ink. The earth turns on its axis.

THE ADVERB.*

99. An **Adverb** is a word which modifies the meaning of a **Verb**, an **Adjective**, or another **Adverb** ; as,

"He acted *wisely*" (Adv. "*wisely*," modifying a Verb).
"The sun is *very* bright" (Adv. "*very*," modifying an Adj.).
"He ran *too* fast" (Adv. "*too*," modifying Adv. "*fast*").

100. Adverbs are used with Verbs to mark the **when**, the **where**, and the **how** of the actions which the Verbs express ; as, "The horsemen *then* rode *away quickly*." Here the Adverbs are *then*, *away*, and *quickly* ; "*then*" marking **when** they rode, "*away*" **where** they rode, and "*quickly*" **how** they rode.

101. Adverbs modifying Adjectives and other Adverbs may be easily known by their answering the question, "**How?**" addressed to the Adjective or Adverb ; as, "John is *very* diligent, *rather* diligent, *exceedingly* diligent, *too* diligent." **Very, rather, exceedingly**, and **too** are Adverbs modifying the Adjective *diligent*, and may be known by their answering the question, "**How diligent?**" In the sentence "John writes well," "*well*" is an Adverb modifying the Verb *writes* ; but by asking "**How well?**" you may find Adverbs to modify "*well*," viz., *very* well, *pretty* well, *exceedingly* well, well *enough*. **Very, pretty, exceedingly**, and **enough**, are Adverbs modifying another Adverb, "*well*."

102. Adverbs are classed as follows :—

Adverbs of **manner**, marking **how** an action is *done* ; as, . . .	well, ill, slowly, quickly, badly, &c.

---

* From Lat. *ad* = to, and verb.

Adverbs of **time**, marking **when**; as, . . .	afterwards, immediately, now, then, when, &c.
Adverbs of **place**, showing the **where** of an action; as, ...	here, there, where, hither, thither, whither, hence, thence, whence, &c.
Adverbs of **degree**, modifying Adjectives and Adverbs; as, . . .	very, too, almost, no, somewhat, much, quite, exceedingly, &c.
Adverbs of **order**, marking **sequence**; as, . .	first or firstly, secondly, thirdly, next, &c.
The **negative** Adverb, .	not.

103. Yes and **no** used as answers, are parsed by some grammarians, not as Adverbs, but as **Word-sentences**; e.g., "Have you dined?" Ans. "No."="I have not dined." "Honest friend, is that ass your own?" Ans. "Yes."="The ass is my own." A Word-sentence is a **sentence compressed** into a single word.

104. Adverbs of manner are formed from Adjectives by adding "**ly**;" thus—

ADJECTIVE.		ADVERB.	ADJECTIVE.		ADVERB.
Just	becomes	*justly.*	*Hard*	becomes	*hardly.*
Bad	"	*badly.*	*Foolish*	"	*foolishly.*
Diligent	"	*diligently.*	*Nice*	"	*nicely.*

By constructing sentences containing Adjectives and their **derived Adverbs**, you may easily learn the different uses of these two parts of speech; as, "That *just* man was not *justly* treated;" "Charles told his *remarkable* story *remarkably* well;" "The plan was a *wise* one, and it was *wisely* executed."

105. The same word may often be used both as an Adjective and as an Adverb:—"He is the *very* man" (*very*, an Adjective). "He is *very* sick" (*very*, an Adverb). "I have a *pretty* flower" (*pretty*, an Adjective). "I have *pretty* good health" (*pretty*, an Adverb). "*The* man told me *the* news" (*the*, a Demonstrative Adjective). "*The* more I know him *the* better I like him" (*the*, an Adverb).

The same word may often be used both as an Adverb and as a Conjunction; *e.g.*, "*Where* are you?" (*where*, an Adverb). "I am standing *where* I was placed" (*where*, *a Conjunction*).

Exercise 11.

(*a.*) Point out all the Adverbs in the following, put each into its proper class, and tell the word it modifies.

I thought it hard enough to turn a grindstone so long on a cold day; but to be now rudely called a little rascal was quite too much for me to bear patiently. It sank very deep in my mind, and often have I thought of it since. When I see a merchant over attentive to his customers, politely begging them to take a little brandy, I always think with myself, "That man has an axe to grind." Come back again soon. Slowly and sadly we laid him down.

(*b.*) Make short sentences, each containing one of the following Adjectives, and an Adverb formed from it.

Severe, harsh, rude, cold, large, sweet, bitter, common, distant, ancient.

THE PREPOSITION.*

106. Prepositions are words placed before Nouns or Pronouns **to connect them with** and **show their relation to** Verbs, Adjectives, or other Nouns or Pronouns; as, "An owl anxious *for* supper, sat *upon* a wall *behind* an old ruin, *with* the intention *of* seizing any mouse or little bird that might come *near* it."

For, upon, behind, with, of, and **near** are Prepositions. "*For*" joins and relates the Noun "*supper*" to the Adjective "*anxious*" (anxious *for* supper); "*upon*" joins and relates the Noun "*wall*" to the Verb "*sat*" (sat *upon* wall); "*behind*" joins and relates the Noun "*ruin*" to the Noun "*wall*" (wall *behind* ruin); "*with*" joins and relates the Noun "*intention*" to the Verb "*sat*" (sat *with* the intention); "*of*" joins and relates the Verbal Noun "*seizing*" to the Noun "*intention*" (intention *of* seizing); and "*near*" joins and relates the Pronoun "*it*" to the Verb "*might come*" (might come *near* it).

Note.—When you parse a word as a Preposition, you are expected to be able to name the words it connects.

107. The Noun or Pronoun following a Preposition is called its **Object**, and is said to be in the **Objective**

* *Derived* from Lat. *præpositus* = placed before.

Case governed by it; as, "He is *at* the *door;*" "He is
Prep. *Object.*
beside *me.*" *Door* and *me* are in the Objective Case,
Prep. *Obj.*
because each is the Object of a Preposition. Prepositions are thus said to govern the Objective Case of Nouns and Pronouns.

108. The nature of the **relations expressed by Prepositions** may be best learned from a few examples. For instance: the floor is *beneath* the ceiling, the ceiling *above* or *over* the floor, the desks *upon* the floor, the boys *in* the desks, the master *among* or *before* the boys, and the boys *beside* each other. **Beneath, above, over, upon, in, among, before,** and **beside** are Prepositions that denote how the objects which are here supposed to be at **rest,** are related to each other.

In the following examples, the Prepositions **along, after, across, up, past, down, into,** and **round,** express relations implying **motion** :—"Go *along* that path and I will go *after* you." "Come *across* the field." "Smoke goes *up* the chimney." "He went *past* the house." "John is going *down* the street." "Come *into* the room." "Magellan sailed *round* the world."

109. Many **Prepositions** may be **used as Adverbs**; as, "Come *along.*" "Go *up.*" "Walk *in.*" "Stand *off.*" "He stayed *outside.*" "The train ran *past.*"

110. Such phrases as—*in spite of, for the sake of, by reason of, by means of,* are called **Compound Prepositions**; as, "He is happy *in spite of* his poverty." "He succeeded *in consequence of* his diligence."

111. The following are some of the most common Prepositions :—

at	below	of	upon
about	between	on	under
above	beyond	over	with
across	by	since	within
after	during	till	without
along	for	to	in behalf of
amidst	from	towards	by means of
before	*in*	through	for the sake of.
behind	*into*	up	in regard to.

Exercise 12.

(*a.*) Pick out the Prepositions in the following, and show what words they connect and relate:—

A writer upon bees mentions that he was once assisted by his maid-servant in hiving a swarm. Being rather fearful, she put a cloth over her head and shoulders. When the bees were shaken off the tree on which they had alighted, the queen probably settled on the cloth; for the whole swarm covered it, and getting under it spread themselves over her face and neck. She was with difficulty kept from running off; but at length her master, having quieted her fears, began to search for the queen.

An old man, famous for his obliging disposition, was riding upon an ass towards the nearest market town; whilst his little boy, almost crippled with walking, was trudging on foot behind him.

(*b.*) Supply the omitted Prepositions:—

James travelled —— Belfast —— Dublin —— train —— Friday. He stayed —— the night —— a hotel, and —— the next morning started —— Kingstown. Taking the steamboat, he sailed —— the channel —— Holyhead —— company —— several passengers. —— Holyhead he took train —— Chester —— the Dee. The train passed —— the Menai Strait, ——, Caernarvonshire, —— a bridge. As he passed —— the Welsh coast, he was so charmed —— the scenery —— him that the time seemed short until he arrived —— Chester.

THE CONJUNCTION.*

112. CONJUNCTIONS *join together* **sentences** and **words**, but their *chief use* is to connect sentences; as "My brother is come, *but* I have not seen him;" "Birds fly *and* fishes swim;" *Neither* James *nor* William came;" "The head *or* chief of a clan;" "A chaise *and* pair."

113. Conjunctions often *seem* to connect words when they *really* join sentences. The two following examples will make this clear:—

1. "John *and* James are good boys."

This is equivalent to the two sentences—"John is a good boy," "James is a good boy," which we unite by the Conjunction *and*, and contract into the expression, "John *and* James *are* good *boys*."

2. *I wish neither* poverty *nor* riches."

---

* *Derived from Lat. conjungere = to join together.*

This is equivalent to the two sentences :—

"I wish not poverty," "I wish not riches,"

which we combine into one by means of the negative Conjunctions *neither* and *nor*, and contract into—"I wish *neither* poverty *nor* riches."

114. The Conjunction *and* really connects words in the following :—

"Her coach *and* four draws up to the door."
"Bread *and* honey is wholesome food."
"The cap cost three-*and*-sixpence."
"'I,' said the sparrow, 'with my bow *and* arrow.'"

The words thus joined express but one idea. See §. 304.

115. Classification of Conjunctions.

Some Conjunctions are **mere connectives**, whilst others mark **various relations** between the sentences which they join ; and this being the principle on which they are classified, we shall illustrate their classification by using *different kinds* of Conjunctions to unite a few pairs of suitable easy sentences ; thus—

(*a*) You help Frank, **and** Frank helps you.
You help Frank, **also** Frank helps you.
You help Frank, **likewise** Frank helps you.
You help Frank, **moreover** Frank helps you.
You help Frank, **besides** Frank helps you.

And, also, likewise, moreover, and *besides,* unite the meanings of the sentences which they connect, and are hence called **Copulative** Conjunctions.

(*b*) You trust Frank, **but** Frank distrusts you.
You trust Frank, **although** Frank distrusts you.
You trust Frank, **yet** Frank distrusts you.
You trust Frank, **notwithstanding** Frank distrusts you.

But, although, yet, and *notwithstanding,* connect sentences *opposed* in meaning, and are hence called **Contrasting** Conjunctions.

(*c*) **Either** you saw Frank, **or** Frank saw you.
You **neither** saw Frank, **nor** did Frank see you.

Either, *neither*, *or*, and *nor*, are called **Distributive** Conjunctions. Notice that *or* follows *either*, and *nor* follows *neither*.

These last two kinds make up the larger class of **Disjunctive** Conjunctions.

(*d*) I help Frank, **because** Frank helps me.
I help Frank, **seeing that** Frank helps me.
I help Frank, **so** Frank helps me.
I help Frank, **therefore** Frank helps me.
Frank works hard, **that** he may succeed.
Frank works hard, **in order that** he may succeed.

Because and *seeing that* are Conjunctions denoting **Cause**; *so* and *therefore* denote **Reason**; *that* and *in order that* denote **Purpose**.

(*e*) Tom would help Frank, **if** he helped Tom.
Tom would help Frank, **provided that** he helped Tom.
Keep Tom and Frank apart, **lest** Frank strike Tom.

If and *provided that* are Conjunctions denoting a **Condition**; *lest* denotes a **Possibility**.

(*f*) I bow to James **when** he bows to me.
John goes **wherever** James goes.
John told me **how** he did it.
John told me **why** he did it.

Conjunctions, such as *when*, *wherever*, *how*, and *why*, express *adverbial relations* of **Time, Place, Manner,** &c., and are therefore called **Adverbial** Conjunctions. They are often called Relative Adverbs. Compare § 73 on the conjunctive use of the Relative Pronoun. This is the easiest way of becoming familiar with the *nature* and *uses* of Conjunctions.

116. Conjunctions are **not always placed between** the sentences they join. Thus you can say—

"I'll stay **if** you go," or "**If** you go I'll stay." "I'll leave **when** you come," or "**When** you come I'll leave." "I saw John **after** the school was dismissed," or "**After** the school was dismissed I saw John."

117. A group of words having the force of a Conjunction is called a **Compound Conjunction**; as, *in order that*, *forasmuch as*, *as well as*, *provided that*, *seeing that*.

Exercise 13.

(*a.*) Point out the Conjunctions in the following, and show the sentences they connect:—

Our clothing, as you know, is made of wool; but this substance is not selected because it imparts warmth. The meeting was not advertised, so there were few present. The crops are good; for the ground is rich, and the weather has been favourable. John and James work hard, therefore they are happy. Mind your business, else you won't succeed. Though he reproved me sharply, yet I can reckon him as a friend. Let us have a walk along the shore before the tide ebbs.

"Though my wallet was scant, I remembered his case,
Nor refused my last crust to his pitiful face;
But he died at my feet on a cold winter's day,
And I played a lament for my poor dog Tray."

(*b.*) Supply the Conjunctions which are omitted:—
Summer is warm —— winter is cold. —— the bear is surly —— it may be tamed. You have never deceived me —— I trust you. —— Jane —— Mary have won prizes. Nothing would live —— the sun did not shine. You should call —— you are in the neighbourhood. John —— James walk —— William drives. Dogs are blind —— they are nine days old. You must know the tables —— you can make progress in arithmetic.

THE INTERJECTION.*

118. **Interjections** are **exclamations** thrown in among other words to call attention; as, *Ho!* or to express some strong sudden feeling; as, *Ah! Oh! Alas! Hurrah!*

Exercise 14.

Point out the **Interjections** in the following:—

Hark! the lark is singing. Lo! the sun is set. What! would you dare to disobey? Oh! the pain was dreadful. Silence! at once. Hush! walk gently. Alas! I never saw him again. Hurrah! on to the charge. Up! up! let us a voyage take. Tush! 'tis some fool has rung and run away. A pretty story, forsooth! Bravo! well done! now only one more effort is needed. Liberty, property, and old England for ever, huzza!

---

* *Derived from* Lat. *interjectus* = thrown among.

SIMPLE PARSING.

119. Simple parsing is the classifying of words according to the *uses they serve* in the sentence.

To do this correctly, you must know well the **definitions** of the eight parts of speech, and the **general meaning** of the passage to be parsed. Before attempting to parse words, you should read the sentence slowly and thoughtfully, and then trust to **common sense** as your guide in detecting the special uses of the different words. Parsing is a mere exercise of common sense, once you know what the parts of speech mean.

Guessing must be avoided above all things, for the same word may be used for different purposes in the same sentence; that is, a word may be a certain part of speech in one place, and a different part of speech in another. The next paragraph will illustrate this.

120. Examples of the same word put to different uses. The word **that** is used as *three* different parts of speech in the sentence, "*That* boy says *that* he has the book *that* you lost." The first *that* is a **Demonstrative Adjective**; the second, a **Conjunction**; the third, a **Relative Pronoun.** *Save* is a **Preposition** in—"All is still, *save* the ceaseless moan of the bubbling rill;" but a **Verb** in "God *save* the Queen." In "His word is *as* good *as* his bond (is)," the first *as* is an **Adverb** modifying *good;* the second, a **Conjunction** connecting the two sentences; and in "He welcomed such *as* came," *as* is a **Relative Pronoun.** In "He is *somewhat* better," *somewhat* is an **Adverb** modifying *better;* but in "I have *somewhat* against thee," the same word is an **Indefinite Pronoun.** "He is not *half* prepared," *half*, an **Adverb**; "*Half* loaf is better than no bread," *half*, an **Adjective**; "The *half* is less than the whole," *half*, a **Noun.** "He is *no* better," *no*, an **Adverb**; "I saw *no* person," *no*, an **Adjective**; "Were you there?" Ans. "*No*" = "I was not there," *no*, a **Word-sentence.** "*What* are you doing?" *what*, an **Interrogative Pronoun**; "*What* country is this?" *what*, an **Adjective**; "I have found *what* I wanted;" *what*, a **Relative Pronoun** = "that which;" "*What* with the roquelaure, and *what* with the weather, it will give your honour your death," *what*, an **Adverb**

(meaning *partly*); " *What!* are all silent?" *what*, an **Interjection**; " *What* is a useful word," *what*, a **Noun.**

MODEL OF SIMPLE PARSING.

121. " Alas! I have been sadly deceived: in early life I was too hopeful, for I received then so many fair promises."

WORD.	CLASS.	BECAUSE
Alas!	an **Interjection**	it is an *exclamation.*
I	a **Pers. Pron.**	it *stands for the name* of a person.
have been deceived	a **Verb** (*pass. voice*)*	it *states.* it states what has been *done to* "I," the Subject.
sadly:	an **Adv.**	it modifies the *Verb* "have been deceived."
in	a **Prep.**	it *connects* and *relates* "*life*" and "*hopeful.*"
early	an **Adj.**	it shows *what* life.
life	a **Noun**	it is a *name.*
was	a **Verb**	it *states.*
too	an **Adv.**	it *modifies* "hopeful," showing *how* hopeful.
hopeful	an **Adj.**	it *describes the person* denoted by "I."
for	a **Conj.**	it *connects the sentences* going before and after.
received	a **Verb.** (*act. voice*)*	it *states.* it states what "I," the subject, *did.*
then	an **Adv.**	it tells *when* "I received."
so	an **Adv.**	it *modifies* the *Adj.* "many."
many	an **Adj.**	it tells the *number* of promises.
fair	an **Adj.**	it tells the *kind* of promises.
promises	a **Noun**	it is a *name.*

INFLECTION.

122. **Inflection** is the **change of form** to which some kinds of words are subject when their application is varied. For example, you would say:—One *lion*, but

* Children should be early taught to distinguish the Active from the Passive Voice.

two *lions;* a *lion's* paw, but two *lions'* paws; the *lion* has a mane, but the *lioness* has none; the boy *writes*, the boy *wrote*, the boy was *writing*, the boy has *written;* a *small* house, a *smaller* house, the *smallest* house. *Lions*, *lion's*, *lions'*, *lioness*, are **Inflections** of the Noun *lion;* *writes*, *wrote*, *writing*, *written*, are inflections of the Verb to *write;* and *smaller*, *smallest*, are inflections of the Adjective *small*.

123. The parts of speech which are inflected are the **Noun**, the **Pronoun**, the **Verb**, the **Adjective**, and the **Adverb**.

INFLECTIONS OF THE NOUN.

124. Nouns are inflected for **Number**, **Gender**, and **Case**.

NUMBER.

125. **Number** is that form of the Noun which denotes *one* or *more than one*.

126. There are two Numbers—the **Singular** and the **Plural**.

The **Singular** (or single) **Number** denotes *one* of anything; as, a *dog*, an *ass*, an *ox*, a *goose*.

The **Plural Number** denotes *more than one;* as, *dogs*, *asses*, *oxen*, *geese*.

127. The Plural Number is usually formed by adding to the Singular the letter **s**; as, *dog*, Plural *dogs;* *slate*, Plural *slates*.

But **es** is added to form the Plural if the Singular ends in *s*, *ss*, *x*, *sh*, *ch* (soft as in church), *z*, and *o* or *y* preceded by a consonant; as,

Singular.	*Plural.*	*Singular.*	*Plural.*
gas	gas*es*.	beech	beech*es*.
ass	ass*es*.	fox	fox*es*.
rush	rush*es*.	topaz	topaz*es*.
potato	potato*es*.	duty	duti*es*.

Notice that duty changes *y* into *i* before adding **es**.

128. When the Singular ends in **f**, as *leaf*, or **fe** as *life*, the **f** usually becomes changed to **v** in the Plural; as,

Singular.	*Plural.*	*Singular.*	*Plural.*
lea*f*	lea*ves*.	li*fe*	li*ves*.
loa*f*	loa*ves*.	wi*fe*	wi*ves*.
shel*f*	shel*ves*.	kni*fe*	kni*ves*.

129. Seven Nouns form the Plural by **changing a vowel** in the middle of the word. They are :—

Singular.	*Plural.*	*Singular.*	*Plural.*
man	men.	goose	geese.
woman	women.	tooth	teeth.
foot	feet.	louse	lice.
		mouse	mice.

130. A few Nouns add **en** to the Singular to make the Plural; as,

Singular.	*Plural.*	*Singular.*	*Plural.*
ox	ox*en*.	child	childr*en*.
brother	brethr*en*.	cow	ki*ne* = cow*en*.

131. Some Nouns have **two Plural forms**, each with a different meaning; as,

Brother, { *brothers*, sons of the same parents. / *brethren*, members of the same society.

Die, { *dies*, for stamping with. / *dice*, for playing.

Genius, { *geniuses*, men of genius. / *genii*, fabulous spirits.

Pea, { *peas*, as four *peas*, denoting number. / *pease*, as a dish of *pease*, denoting quantity.

Penny, { *pennies*, as four *pennies*, denoting number. / *pence*, as four *pence*, denoting **value**.

132. Some Nouns, as *salmon*, *deer*, *sheep*, have **no Plural form**, although they are used in both numbers. Thus we say one *sheep* or ten *sheep*, but not ten sheeps; one *deer* or ten *deer*, but not ten deers.

133. The following kinds of Nouns are used only in the Singular :—

(*a*) **Names of materials** ; as, *gold*, *silver*, *brass*.

(*b*) **Names of qualities** ; as, *strength*, *goodness*.

(*c*) **Proper Nouns** ; as, *William*, *Ireland*, *Dublin*.

Proper Nouns, as such, cannot be used in the Plural, a Proper Noun being the name of an individual; as *Henry*, *Mary*. But when such names are used to denote **classes**, as, a *Cromwell*, the *Henrys*, the *Marys*, they may be Plural; but they are then Common Nouns.

134. The words—*scissors*, *tongs*, *trowsers*, &c., have **no Singular form** ; we never say a *scissor*, a *trowser*, a *tong*. Such Nouns are *naturally* Plural.

135. Adopted foreign Nouns, as a rule, keep their native Plurals. Their tendency, however, is to assume the regular English Plural, and thus we have such words as *cherub* with **two** Plural forms—*cherubs* and *cherubim*.

136. The following are foreign Nouns with their native Plurals :—

Singular.	*Plural.*	*Singular.*	*Plural.*
datum	**data (Lat.)**	**cherub**	**cherubim (Heb.)**
monsieur	messieurs (Fr.)	conversazione	conversazioni (It.)
phenomenon	phenomena (Gr).	madame	mesdames (Fr.)
bandit	banditti (Ital.)	locus	loci (Lat.)

Exercise 15.

(*a*.) Tell the **Plural** of the following Nouns in the Singular :—

Wife, hat, goose, ox, button, top, ass, horse, cow (two plurals), wolf, an alms, brother (two plurals), knife, potato, city, cargo, calf, day, guinea, penny (two plurals), box.

(*b*.) Tell the **Number** of the following Nouns :—

Mice, women, deer, daisy, rubies, sheep, kine, cattle, vale, sheaves, workmen, cherubim, tongues, madame, phenomena, messieurs, goodness, strength, feet, mistress, tongs, cheese, trees, breezes, brush, oxen, swine, John, group, lungs, a deer, an apparatus.

(*c*.) **Correct the following, as necessary** :—

Feets, *boots*, treeses, breezes, handses, oxes, horses, shoe, shoeses, *trowsers*, *mouses*, a teeth, a mice, almses, scissor, monsieurs.

GENDER.

137. Gender is that form of a Noun or Pronoun which denotes whether we are speaking of **males** or **females**, or **things without life**.

138. The names of males are said to be of the **Masculine Gender**; as, *father*, *brother*, *king*.

139. The names of females are said to be of the **Feminine Gender**; as, *mother*, *sister*, *queen*.

140. The names of lifeless things are said to be of the **Neuter Gender**; as, *pen*, *desk*, *rock*.

141. Names that may be applied to either males or females are said to be of the **Common Gender**; as, *teacher*, *parent*, *pupil*.

The word *gender* comes from LAT. *genus* = kind.

142. The Masculine and Feminine Genders **are distinguished in three ways**, as follows:—

1. By a different word; as—

Masculine.	*Feminine.*	*Masculine.*	*Feminine.*
bachelor	maid, spinster.	hart	roe.
beau	belle.	horse	mare.
boar	sow.	husband	wife.
boy	girl.	king	queen.
bridegroom	bride.	lad	lass.
brother	sister.	lord	lady.
buck	doe.	man	woman.
bull	cow.	master	mistress.
bullock, ox, steer	heifer.	nephew	niece.
		papa	mamma.
cock	hen.	ram	ewe.
colt	filly.	sir	madam.
dog	bitch.	sloven	slut.
drake	duck.	son	daughter.
earl	countess.	stag	hind.
father	mother.	swain	nymph.
friar or monk	nun.	uncle	aunt.
gander	goose.	widower	widow.
gentleman	lady.	wizard	witch.

2. By a different termination; as—

abbot	abbess.	jew	jewess.
actor	actress.	lion	lioness.
ambassador	ambassadress.	marquess } marquis }	marchioness.
author	authoress.	mayor	mayoress.
baron	baroness.	patron	patroness.
benefactor	benefactress.	peer	peeress.
conductor	conductress.	poet	poetess.
count	countess.	priest	priestess.
czar	czarina.	prince	princess.
deacon	deaconess.	prophet	prophetess.
duke	duchess.	protector	protectress.
elector	electress.	shepherd	shepherdess.
emperor	empress.	songster	songstress.
enchanter	enchantress.	sorcerer	sorceress.
executor	executrix.	sultan	{ sultaness. sultana.
giant	giantess.	testator	testatrix.
governor	governess.	tiger	tigress.
heir	heiress.	traitor	traitress.
hero	heroine.	viscount	viscountess.
host	hostess.		
hunter	huntress.		

3. By putting a Masculine or Feminine word before or after a Noun of the Common Gender; as—

man-servant	maid-servant.	he-ass	she-ass.
male-child	female-child.	he-bear	she-bear.
cock-sparrow	hen-sparrow.	turkey-cock	turkey-hen.
he-goat	she-goat.	pea-cock	pea-hen.

Exercise 16.

(*a.*) Tell the **Feminine** of the following Nouns:—

Horse, boy, count, priest, lad, brother, ram, nephew, bullock, drake, sultan, czar, stag, baron, nephew, pea-cock, hero, king, emperor, lion, cock-sparrow, giant, husband.

(*b.*) *Distinguish the following Nouns as of the Masculine, Feminine, Common, or Neuter Gender:—*

Teacher, table, chair, cow, parent, tiger, queen, minister, bird, prince, czarina, colt, book, month, drake, daughter, poet, carpenter, scholar, slate, child, father, sun.

CASE.

143. A Noun (or Pronoun) may be employed in a sentence as—

(*a*) The **Subject of the Verb** (see § 87); as, "*Honey* is sweet." "*He* was praised."

Subj. Verb. *Subj. Verb.*

(*b*) The **Direct Object of a Transitive Verb** (see § 88); as,

"Bees gather *honey*." "John praised *him*."
(gather: *Trans. Verb.*; honey: *Direct Obj.*; praised: *Trans. Verb.*; him: *Direct Obj.*)

(*c*) The **Object of a Preposition** (see § 107); as,

"Jack is in the *house*." "Tom is with *him*."
(in: *Prep.*; house: *Obj. of Prep.*; with: *Prep.*; him: *Obj. of Prep.*)

(*d*) The **Name of the Possessor of something**; as,

"A *man's* hat." "*John's* farm." "*My* book."
(*Possessor.* *Possessor.* *Possessor.*)

These different *uses* of the Noun (or Pronoun) are called **Cases**. Case, however, is often defined as **the form a Noun (or Pronoun) assumes, in order** *to denote its relation* **to some other word in the same sentence.**

144. Nouns have three Cases:—

1. The **Nominative** (or Subjective) Case.
2. The **Objective** Case.
3. The **Possessive** Case.

The Nominative and Objective of English Nouns are spelt alike, and must be distinguished from each other by the *position* and *use* of the Noun in the sentence.

Personal Pronouns have forms for each of the three Cases.

145. When a Noun (or Pronoun) is made the **Subject of a Verb**, it is said to be in the **Nominative Case**; as,

1. "*Frank* leaps." (Frank: *Subj.*; leaps: *Verb.*)
2. "*Bob* was struck." (Bob: *Subj.*; was struck: *Verb.*)
3. "Does *Jane* sing?" (Does: *Verb.*; Jane: *Subj.*; sing: *Verb.*)
4. "Be (*thou, ye,* or *you*) silent." (Be: *Verb.*; thou, ye, or you: *Subj.*)

1. *Frank* is Nominative Case to the Verb *leaps.*
2. *Bob* is Nominative Case to the Verb *was struck.*
3. *Jane* is Nominative Case to the Verb *does sing.*
4. *Thou, ye,* or *you* is Nominative Case to the Verb *be.*

Notice that *Frank* and *Bob* precede their Verbs in the *asserting* sentences (1) and (2); but that in the question,

"Does Jane sing?" and in the *command*, "Be (thou, ye, or you) silent," the Nominative Case comes second in order. The Nominative to a commanding Verb is always *thou*, *ye*, or *you*: it may be expressed, as "Be *ye* perfect;" but it is usually understood.

The word *Nominative* means *naming*. The Nominative Case *names* the *Subject* of the Verb, and is therefore often called the *Subjective Case*.

146. When a Noun (or Pronoun) is the **Direct Object** of a Transitive Verb, or the **Object** of a Preposition expressed or understood, it is said **to be** in the **Objective Case**; as,

1. "Jack built a *house*."
   built = *Trans. Verb.*; house = *Direct Obj.*

2. "The pen is in my *hand*."
   in = *Prep.*; hand = *Obj. of Prep.*

3. "James bought his *son* a *book*" = "James bought (*for*) his *son* a *book*."
   for = *Prep.*; son = *Obj. of Prep.*; book = *Direct Obj. of bought.*

1. *House* is the Direct Object of the Trans. Verb *built*, therefore *house* is Objective Case governed by the Verb *built*.
2. *Hand* is the Object of the Preposition *in*, therefore *hand* is Objective Case governed by the Preposition *in*.
3. *Son* is the Object of the Preposition *for* (understood), and is therefore Objective Case governed by *for*. This is called the **Indirect Object** of the Verb, which often corresponds to the *Dative Case in Latin*. *Book* is the Direct Object, or Objective Case governed by *bought*.

147. When a **Relative Pronoun** is a Direct Object, it naturally **goes before** the Verb which governs it; as, "This is the house *which* Jack built." (which = *Direct Obj.*; built = *Verb.*) "*Which* Jack *built*" = "*Jack* built *which*." Remember this, and also *what is meant* by the Indirect Object.

148. When a Noun (or Pronoun) denotes the possessor of something, it is said to be in the **Possessive Case**; as, *Mary's* dress, *Joseph's* coat.
possessor. *possessor.*

This is the only Case of English Nouns that may be known from the spelling of the word; the others must be thought out.

149. The Possessive Case is formed as follows:—

(*a.*) If the Nominative Case does **not** end in **s**, the Possessive is formed by adding to the Nominative (**'s**); as, dog, *dog's*; men, *men's.*
Nom. *Poss.* *Nom.* *Poss.*

(*b.*) But if the Nominative ends in **s** or an **s sound**, the Possessive is usually formed by adding (') only; as, boys, *boys'*; Moses, *Moses'*; justice, *justice'.*
Nom. *Poss.* *Nom.* *Poss.* *Nom.* *Poss.*

Exceptions.—Proper names consisting of not more than two syllables, and ending in **s**, form the Possessive by adding **'s** when the added sound (**es**) is not unpleasant to the ear; as, "*James's* pen," "*Thomas's* book," "*Chambers's* Journal." We also write, an *ass's* cart, an *actress's* robes, the *Prince of Wales's* carriage.

Notice that 's, in such cases, is pronounced **es**.

150. The **Possessive Case** may, usually without altering the sense, be **changed to the Objective** governed by the Preposition *of*; as, "*William's* ball" = "The ball *of William.*" The Possessive of **Neuter Nouns** is generally expressed in that way: we *say*, "the leg *of a chair*," not "A *chair's* leg;" but the *regular* form is used in such expressions as, "A *week's* wages," "A *year's* growth." "A *summer's* sun."

151. When a Noun stands as the name of a person addressed it is said to be in the "**Nominative of Address**;" as, "O *father*, I have got a prize!" "*James*, answer me this question."
Nom. of Address. *Nom. of Address.*

This Case *corresponds* to the Vocative in Latin, and *should be called* the **Vocative Case**.

There is also a **Nominative of Exclamation** ; as,

"O the *famine* and the *fever!*
O the *wasting* of the famine !
O the *blasting* of the fever!
O the *wailing* of the children !
O the *anguish* of the women !"

Famine, fever, wasting, blasting, wailing, and *anguish,* are in the Nominative of Exclamation.

NOTE.—Nouns thus used partake of the nature of Interjections.

152. Nouns are thus **declined** :—

	Singular.	*Plural.*
Nom. and *Obj.* . . .	Father.	Fathers.
Poss.	Father's.	Fathers'.
Nom. and *Obj.* . . .	Man.	Men.
Poss.	Man's.	Men's.

Nom. and *Obj.*	Moses.	*Nom.* and *Obj.*	James.
Poss.	Moses'.	*Poss.*	James's.

Compound or Descriptive Nouns, and Pronouns consisting of two or more words, are thus declined :—

Nom. and *Obj.* . . .	Sullivan, Brothers and Co.
Poss.	Sullivan, Brothers and Co.'s.
Nom. and *Obj.* . . .	Moore and Robinson.
Poss.	Moore and Robinson's.
Nom. and *Obj.* . . .	Any one else.
Poss.	Any one else's.

Here, as you may observe, the rule is to put the sign of the Possessive after the last word.

Exercise 17.

(*a.*) *Decline the following Nouns* :—

Fox, boy, lady, day, apple, moon, mouse, thief, wife, valley, bank, purse, soldier, enemy, grocer, potato, cat, gardener, summer, Apostle, Mr. Stubbs, Demosthenes.

(*b.*) *Insert the Apostrophe* ;—

The ladies waiting-room ; the boys playground ; Jacks new top ; *a girls ten fingers ;* ten girls fingers ; two years earnings ; the *summers sun ;* the years last rose ; the carpenters society ; ten *mens work ;* a hares fur ; a ladys maid ; ten clerks salaries ; Sullivans Grammar; Joyces Hand-Book; four lions dens; two bears paws; a bears fur.

(c.) *Correct where Apostrophe is wrongly inserted:—*

My brothers' pen; my sister's slate; two babie's dresses; the hunter's horse; the gooses' feathers; Johns' son's coat; ten soldiers' arms; Williams' friends' father's house; two day's wages; two cat's paws; a horses' mane; two horses' manes; The Apostle's Creed.

(d.) *Distinguish the Nominative (or Subjective) from the Objective Case in the following sentences:—*

The cat killed a rat. The house was burnt. There is a man at the door. I hear a step on the stair. Many hands make light work. The child has a toy. Find the answer to that sum (supply the *Nominative* after *find*). James gave John his pen (supply *to* after *gave*). Remember your Creator in the days of your youth. How many articles make a dozen? The ship was lost; but the crew was saved. The boy tore his coat. His mother reproved him. The idle boy was punished by his teacher. The weather has changed since yesterday. My father sold a horse. The farmer is going to the fair to buy two cows. Good boys love their teachers. Good teachers encourage their pupils. Are those pears good?

(e.) *Change the following Possessives into Objectives with of:—*

The man's boots; the boy's collar; a duck's egg; a horse's hoof; ten girls' dresses; John's farm; the master's desk; a sailor's jacket; two ships' crews; the scholars' advantage; the soldier's sword; two rivers' banks.

INFLECTION OF PRONOUNS.

153. Personal Pronouns have **Person, Number, Gender,** and **Case.**

154. Person denotes—

(*a*) The **speaker**; as, *I, me.*
(*b*) The **person addressed**; as, *thou, thee.*
(*c*) The **person or thing spoken of**; as, *he, it, one.*

(See § 66 for the meaning of *First, Second,* and *Third Person.*)

Gender is distinguished in the **Third Person only**; as, *he* (Masculine), *she* (Feminine), *it* (Neuter).

I (First Person) and *thou* (Second Person) are of the ***Common Gender.***

155. The Personal Pronouns are thus **declined** :—

First Person.

Singular.		*Plural.*	
Nom.	I.	*Nom.*	We.
Poss.	My or Mine.	*Poss.*	Our or Ours.
Obj.	Me.	*Obj.*	Us.

Second Person.

Nom.	Thou.	*Nom.*	Ye or You.
Poss.	Thy or Thine.	*Poss.*	Your or Yours.
Obj.	Thee.	*Obj.*	You, Ye (seldom).

Third Person.

Masculine.

Nom.	He.	*Nom.*	They.
Poss.	His.	*Poss.*	Their or Theirs.
Obj.	Him.	*Obj.*	Them.

Feminine.

Nom.	She.	*Nom.*	They.
Poss.	Her or Hers.	*Poss.*	Their or Theirs.
Obj.	Her.	*Obj.*	Them.

Neuter.

Nom.	It.	*Nom.*	They.
Poss.	Its.	*Poss.*	Their or Theirs.
Obj.	It.	*Obj.*	Them.

156. The **Possessive forms** of the Personal Pronouns are used (1) as **Possessive Adjectives**, and (2) as **Possessive Pronouns.**

A Possessive Adjective is always **followed by a Noun,** and denotes a **Possessor.** The forms thus used are—**my, thy, his, her, its, our, your, their,** and sometimes **mine** and **thine**; as, *my* book, *their* pens, *his* cap, *thine* eye. (See § 57.)

157. A **Possessive Pronoun** may be known thus :—

1. **It is never followed by a Noun**; *e.g.*, "The book is *yours.*"
2. *It* denotes both **a possessor** and the **thing possessed**; as, "That pen is better than *mine*" (*mine* = *my pen*).

3. It can be made—
   (*a*) The **Subject of a Verb**; as, "*Yours* are as good as *his* (are)."
   (*b*) The **Object of a Verb**; as, "They have lost *theirs*."
   (*c*) The **Object of a Preposition**; as, "Take half of *mine*."

The words that can be used as Possessive Pronouns are—**mine, thine, his, hers, its, ours, yours, theirs, my own, his own, her own, their own,** &c. **Own** is added to mark emphasis.

158. The **Indefinite Personal Pronoun** "*one*" is thus declined:—

Masculine and *Feminine*.

Singular.		*Plural.*	
Nom.	One.	*Nom.*	Ones.
Poss.	One's.	*Poss.*	Ones'.
Obj.	One.	*Obj.*	Ones.

One and its Plural **ones**, when qualified by Adjectives, should be parsed as **Nouns**; as, "A good *one*;" "The little *ones*."

159. Relative Pronouns are thus declined:—

Singular and *Plural*.

Nom.	Who	*Masculine* and *Feminine*
Poss.	Whose	
Obj.	Whom	

Singular and *Plural*.

Nom.	Which	*Neuter*.
Poss.	Whose	
Obj.	Which	

Singular and *Plural*.

Nom.	That	*Masculine, Feminine,* or *Neuter*.
Poss.	(*wanting*)	
Obj.	That	

NOTE.—The Relative *that* is indeclinable, but some regard *whose* as a borrowed Possessive.

160. The **Interrogative Pronouns** WHO? and WHICH? are declined like the **Relatives** *who* and *which*. WHAT? suffers no inflection.

161. The **Demonstrative Pronouns** *this* and *that* are inflected for Number thus :—

Singular.	*Plural.*
This.	These.
That.	Those.

162. Pronouns must be of the same **Number** and **Gender** as the Nouns for which they stand. Remember this when correcting Exercise (*b*).

Exercise 18.

(*a.*) Tell the **Case, Number,** and **Gender** of the following Pronouns :—

Mine, him, them, its, hers, he, who, whom, thou, whose, thine, yours, them, theirs, I, that, me, his, us, she.

(*b.*) The Pronouns in the following sentences are incorrectly used. Correct them.

He is a good cow; it gives much milk. I hear the train; she is coming. That tree is very large; he was planted fifty years ago. Dogs love her masters. Boys should respect his teachers. My watch cost thirty pounds; she keeps good time. She is a good fiddle. The girl has lost their book; let us try to find him for it. Teachers should have his pupils in subjection, else it will not succeed in teaching him. The pump was injured; but the plumber has repaired her.

INFLECTION OF ADJECTIVES AND ADVERBS.

163. A number of objects may possess the same quality or attribute in different degrees, thus :—

"Carn Tual is a *high* mountain."
"Mont Blanc is a *higher* mountain than Carn Tual."
"Mount Everest is the *highest* mountain of the three."
"Mount Everest is the *highest* mountain in the world."
"William is *diligent.*"
"Frank is *more diligent* than William."
"Sam is the *most diligent* of the three; in fact, he is *the most diligent* boy in the school."

Such forms as high, higher, highest, diligent, more diligent, most diligent, are called **Degrees of Comparison.**

164. There are three Degrees of Comparison: the **Positive**, the **Comparative**, and the **Superlative.**

165. The **Positive Degree** is the **simple form** of the Adjective, and merely denotes that an object possesses a certain quality or attribute; as, "a *rich* man," "*much* corn."

166. The **Comparative Degree** denotes that two objects or groups are compared, and that one of them possesses a certain quality in a **higher degree** than the other; as, "John is *richer* than James." "Your brothers are *taller* than mine."

Notice that the Conjunction *than* follows the Comparative Degree.

167. The **Superlative Degree** denotes that one object possesses a certain quality in a **higher degree than all others** compared with it; as, "Thomas is the *richest* man in town." "Russia is the *largest* country in Europe."

Observe that the Superlative may be changed to the Comparative Degree thus: "Smith is the *tallest* boy at the school" = "Smith is *taller* than any other boy at the school."

168. Adjectives of **one syllable** form the Comparative Degree by adding **er**, and the Superlative by adding **est**, to the Positive; as, just, just*er*, just*est*. But if the

Pos. Comp. Sup.

Positive ends in **e**, as '*wise*,' **r** and **st** only are added; as, wise, wise*r*, wise*st*.

Pos. Comp. Sup.

When the Adjective is a word of **more than one syllable**, the Comparative is formed by prefixing **more**, and the Superlative by prefixing **most**, to the Positive; as, attentive, *more* attentive, *most* attentive.

Pos. Comp. Sup.

Note.—The former is called the **Inflectional**, *and the latter, the* **Adverbial** *method of comparing Adjectives.*

169. **Adjectives of two syllables** ending in **e, y, ow,** and **er,** may be compared both ways; as,

Pos.	*Comp.*	*Sup.*	*Comp.*	*Sup.*
able	abler	ablest	more able	most able
happy	happier	happiest	more happy	most happy
shallow	shallower	shallowest	more shallow	most shallow
tender	tenderer	tenderest	more tender	most tender

170. The following Adjectives are **irregular**:—

Positive.	*Comparative.*	*Superlative.*
good	better	best
bad, evil, ill	worse	worst
little	less	least
much, many	more	most
old	older / elder	oldest / eldest
far	farther	farthest
[forth, *adv.*]	further	furthest
fore	former	foremost *or* first
hind	hinder	hindmost
[in, *prep.*]	inner	inmost, innermost
[out, *adv.*]	outer / utter	outmost, utmost / uttermost
late	later, latter	latest, last
[neath, *prep.*]	nether	nethermost
[up, *prep.*]	upper	upmost, uppermost
nigh	nigher	nighest, next

171. Observe that a **comparison of Diminution** is expressed by means of the Adverbs **less** and **least**; as, a valiant man, a *less* valiant man, the *least* valiant man.

Pos. *Comp.* *Sup.*

172. **Adverbs**, like Adjectives, have three Degrees of Comparison. Most of them are compared by prefixing **more** and **most** to the Positive; as, gladly, *more* gladly, *most* gladly.

173. Some Adverbs are compared by **er** and **est**; as *soon, sooner, soonest; often, oftener, oftenest.*

The following are **irregular** :—

Positive.	*Comparative*	*Superlative.*
well	better	best
badly *or* ill	worse	worst
much	more	most
little	less	least
far	farther	farthest
forth	further	furthest

174. Double forms of the Comparative and Superlative are not to be used. You would not say, "London is a *more larger* city than Paris; it is, in fact, the *most largest* city in the world;" but, "London is a *larger* city than Paris; it is, in fact, the *largest* city in the world."

Exercise 19.

(*a.*) Tell the **Comparative** and **Superlative** of each of the following Adjectives and Adverbs in the Positive Degree :—

ADJECTIVES.

Excellent, fine, troublesome, dark, narrow, beautiful, large, spacious, stormy, intelligible, dangerous, unwelcome, pretty, cheap, honourable, handsome, dutiful.

ADVERBS.

Excellently, narrowly, beautifully, soon, largely, often, prettily, honourably, handsonely, badly, cheaply, little, tenderly.

(*b.*) Tell the **Degrees of Comparison** of the Adjectives in the following :—

Ireland has a more humid climate than England. William is diligent. He is in the inner office. The outer margin. The skilful general. The utmost limits. An extra quantity. A more obedient son. Deeds are better than words. A most obliging neighbour. A most entertaining story. John took a more decided course. This is sad news. A more likely candidate. The least likely candidate Most noble Festus.

(*c.*) Correct the folowing :—

The baddest writer. The most correctest speaker. The lesser angle. The worser kind. A more beautifuler landscape. The goodest boy in the shool. The entertainingest story. There could not be a more diigenter girl. John is the attentivest pupil in the school. The mst obligingest man.

INFLECTIONS OF THE VERB.

175. Verbs are inflected for **Number, Person, Tense, Mood,** and **Voice.**

NUMBER AND PERSON.

176. A Verb is **Singular** when its **Nominative is Singular**, and **Plural** when its **Nominative is Plural**; as, he *walks*, they *walk*, John *walked*, they *walked*.

Sing. *Plur.* *Sing.* *Plur.*

177. A Verb is of the **First**, the **Second**, or the **Third Person** according as its **Nominative** is of the **First**, the **Second**, or the **Third Person**; as, I *walk*, thou *walkest*,

1st pers. *2d pers.*

he *walks*, I *walked*, thou *walkedst*, he *walked*.

3d pers. *1st pers.* *2d pers.* *3d. pers.*

178. Notice that the Second Person Singular ends in **est** and **st** in "thou walk*est*," "thou walked*st*," and that the Third Person Singular ends in **s** in "he walk*s*;" but has no special ending (or inflection) in "he walked." English Verbs are inflected for Number and Person, only in the **Second** and **Third Person Singular** of the simple Present Tense, and in the **Second Person Singular** of the simple Past.

TENSE.*

179. Tense is that form of the Verb which indicates **Time.**

Time may be viewed as **Present, Past,** or **Future,** and Verbs have three chief Tenses corresponding with these divisions, viz., the **Present Tense** which refers to time now passing; as, I *write*, I *am writing*; the **Past Tense** which refers to time past; as, I *wrote*, I *was writing*; and the **Future Tense** denoting time to come; as, I *shall write*, I *shall be writing*.

But Tenses often denote more than mere Time; they can also tell the **States of Actions.** Read carefully the *next paragraph.*

---

* **Latin,** ***tempus*** **= time.**

180. States of Actions.—When I say "The maid *is milking* the cow," "The maid *was milking* the cow," "The maid *will be milking* the cow," I think of the action of milking as *going on* or Progressive; but when I say "The maid *has milked* the cow," "The maid *had milked* the cow," "The maid *will have milked* the cow," I think of the action of milking as *finished* or Perfect. **This explains what is meant by the two States of actions —the Progressive and the Perfect.**

When a Tense defines the State of an action as *going on*, it is a **Progressive Tense**; as, "Tom *is playing, was playing*, or *will be playing* ball."

A **Perfect Tense** defines the State of an action as *finished* or *complete;* as, "The ship *has sailed*," "The ship *had sailed* (before I left)," "The ship *will have sailed* (before two o'clock to-morrow)."

An **Indefinite Tense** does *not* define the State of an action, but merely shows that it is Present, Past, or Future; as, "The bird *sings* or *does sing*," "James *walked* up the street," "Tom *will please* his employer." Tenses have three States—the **Progressive**, the **Perfect**, and the **Indefinite** (or *undefined* State).

181. A **Simple Tense** consists of *one* word. English Verbs have only two Simple Tenses—one Present, the other Past; as, Present, I *hear;* Past, I *heard:* Present, I *call;* Past, I *called*. The simple Past Tense of Regular Verbs, is formed by adding *d* or *ed* to the Simple Present, as in the examples just given.

A **Compound Tense** consists of *two* or *more* words; as, I *had called;* I *shall have called*. The last word of a Compound Tense is the **Principal Verb**; the preceding word or words are **Auxiliary** or **helping Verbs**. In *shall have called*, **called** is the Principal Verb, **shall** and **have** are Auxiliaries.

182. THE FORMS OF THE PRESENT TENSE.

Present Indefinite.

Singular.	*Plural.*
I **write** *or* **do write.**	*We* **write** *or* **do write.**
Thou **writest** *or* **dost write.**	*Ye or You* **write** *or* **do write.**
He **writes** *or* **does write.**	*They* **write** or **do write.**

PRESENT PROGRESSIVE.

Singular.	*Plural.*
I **am writing.**	***We*** **are writing.**
Thou **art writing.**	***Ye or You*** **are writing.**
He **is writing.**	***They*** **are writing.**

PRESENT PERFECT.

Singular.	*Plural.*
I **have written.**	***We*** **have written.**
Thou **hast written.**	***Ye or You*** **have written.**
He **has written.**	***They*** **have written.**

This Tense denotes an action **finished now** ; hence its name. "I *have dined*" = "I *have* (just now) *dined*."

The Present Perfect Tense is formed, as you may see, by putting **Have, Hast,** or **Has** before the Past Participle of another Verb. But **Verbs of motion,** as, '*To Go*,' '*To Come*,' &c., have two forms for this Tense—the usual one, as given above, and the following, which is formed thus: I (*am*) *come*, Thou (*art*) *come*, He (*is*) *come*, We (*are*) *come*, &c. Call '*is come*,' '*are come*,' &c., the **Present Perfect Tense** of the Verb '*To Come*;' and remember that it is not a form of the Passive Voice, for '*Come*' is an Intransitive Verb.

PRESENT PERFECT PROGRESSIVE. *I* **have been writing.** *Thou* **hast been writing.** *He* **has been writing, &c.**

183. THE FORMS OF THE PAST TENSE.

PAST INDEFINITE.

Singular.	*Plural.*
I **wrote** *or* **did write.**	***We*** **wrote** *or* **did write.**
Thou **wrotest** *or* **didst write.**	***Ye or You*** **wrote** *or* **did write.**
He **wrote** *or* **did write.**	***They*** **wrote** *or* **did write.**

PAST PROGRESSIVE.

Singular.	*Plural.*
I **was writing.**	***We*** **were writing.**
Thou **wast writing.**	***Ye or You*** **were writing.**
He **was writing.**	***They*** **were writing.**

PAST PERFECT.

Singular.	*Plural.*
I **had written.**	***We*** **had written.**
Thou **hadst written.**	***Ye or You*** **had written.**
He **had written.**	***They*** **had written.**

This Tense denotes an action **finished in the Past**; hence its name; as, I *had left* before you called.

The Past Perfect Tense is formed, as you may see, by putting **Had** or **Hadst** before the Past Participle of another Verb. But some Verbs of motion may also form this Tense thus: "I (*was*) *come*, Thou (*wast*) *come*, He (*was*) *come*." "He *was come*" = "He *had come*."

184. The **Future Tense** is formed by using **Shall** and **Will** before the Infinitive of other Verbs, the sign '**to**' being suppressed; as, 'I *shall go*' = 'I shall (to) go,' 'You *will be sent*' = 'You will (to) be *sent*.'

Learn this:—**Shall** in the *First* Person, and **Will** in the *Second* and *Third*, denote **mere futurity**. **Will** in the *First* Person denotes **purpose**—'I *will* go' = 'I *mean* to go.' **Shall** in the *Second* and *Third* implies **duty, obligation, authority**, &c., and is often equivalent to a command; *e.g.*, "Thou *shalt not kill*" = "Thou *must not kill*," or "Thou *art commanded not to kill*." "He *shall leave* my house" = "He *will be obliged to leave* my house." **Shall** originally meant '*to owe*,' a meaning which you may still trace in its Past Tense, "I *should*" = "I *ought*." **Will** means *wish* or *pleasure*. (See § 226 to § 228 inclusive for further information on Shall and Will.)

185. THE FORMS OF THE **FUTURE** TENSE.

UNEMPHATIC FUTURE TENSE.

(*Denoting mere futurity.*)

	Singular.	Plural.
INDEFINITE	***I* shall write.**	***We* shall write.**
	***Thou* wilt write.**	***Ye* or *You* will write.**
	***He* will write.**	***They* will write.**

PROGRESSIVE. ***I* shall be writing, *Thou* wilt be writing**, &c.

EMPHATIC FUTURE TENSE.

(*Denoting purpose, duty, obligation, &c.*)

	Singular.	Plural.
INDEFINITE	***I* will write.**	***We* will write.**
	***Thou* shalt write.**	***Ye* or *You* shall write.**
	***He* shall write.**	***They* shall write.**

PROGRESSIVE. ***I* will be writing, *Thou* shalt be writing**, *&c.*

FUTURE PERFECT TENSE.
(*Unemphatic.*)

Singular.	*Plural.*
I **shall have written.**	*We* **shall have written.**
Thou **wilt have written.**	*Ye or You* **will have written.**
He **will have written.**	*They* **will have written.**

EMPHATIC FORM. *I* **will have written,** *Thou* **shalt have written,** &c.

This Tense denotes an action **to be finished** in the Future; hence its name; *e.g.*, "I *shall have studied* Fractions by next Easter."

The Future Perfect Tense is formed, as you may see, by putting **Shall have** and **Will have** before the Past Participle of other Verbs.

Exercise 20.

(*a.*) Tell the **Number** and **Person** of the Verbs in the following:—

I moved the chair. John is idle. They have received their prizes. Thou wilt come. Birds build nests. You (or ye) hear what he has said. I am your teacher. Thou art my pupil. We are doing our work. A hare can run fast. Greyhounds can run faster. She lost her needle. Have you found it? Cows give milk. The sheep was grazing in the field. Sheep give us wool.

(*b.*) Tell the **Tenses** of the following Verbs, and also of those in the last Exercise:—The wind blew. The dew was falling. Mary is writing. John has read the book you gave him. James will start this evening for London. The master will be teaching to-morrow. Bees work in the sunshine. Did you hear the thunder? Tom is playing cricket. Before John returns, the school will have closed for the holidays. I had finished my exercise before you came in. Frank has been reading all day. Fishes swim.

(*c.*) Distinguish the **Unemphatic** and **Emphatic Future.** We shall surely die. Ye shall not surely die. You shall do my will. The Lord will come; the earth shall quake. I shall likely meet you in town. He will endeavour to do his duty. Thou shalt not steal. I will join my ship; but I fear I shall be drowned. My servant shall go to-morrow. I will do what you ask. Thou shalt love thy neighbour as thyself. We shall get out of school at three o'clock.

MOOD.*

186. MOOD is that form of the Verb which shows the ***mode or manner*** in which an action is expressed.

---

* Lat. *modus* = a manner.

187. Verbs have five Moods—the **Indicative**, the **Imperative**, the **Subjunctive**, the **Potential**, and the **Infinitive**.

188. The **Indicative** Mood **simply states a fact**; as, "Cows *eat* grass;" or **asks a direct question**; as, "*Do* cows *eat* grass?"

'*Eat*' simply states a fact, and '*do eat*' asks a direct question; therefore, '*eat*' and '*do eat*' are in the Indicative Mood.

189. When a Verb expresses a **command** or an **entreaty**, it is in the **Imperative** Mood; as, "*Go* away." "*Come* back." "*Forgive* me." *Go*, *come*, and *forgive* are in the Imperative Mood. The Imperative Mood is generally used in the Second Person with "*thou*" or "*you*" as Subject (usually understood). It is sometimes employed in the Third; as, "Thy kingdom *come*." "Thy money *perish* with thee."

"*Be* Yarrow's stream unseen, unknown."

It may be used even in the First Person; *e.g.*—

"'Now *tread* we a measure!' said young Lochinvar."

Notice that "*Thy money perish* with thee" = "*Let thy money perish* with thee;" and "Now *tread we* a measure" = "Now *let us tread* a measure." In these equivalent expressions, '*let*' should be parsed as the *Imperative* Mood, Second Person; and '*perish*' and '*tread*,' the *Infinitive* following '*let*.'

190. The **Subjunctive** Mood **expresses a condition**, a **doubt**, or a **possibility**; as, "If *I were* John I would act otherwise." "Resist temptation lest it *overcome* you."

Subj. Mood. / *Subj. Mood.*

This Mood is distinguished from the Indicative by its **want of inflections**; thus, in the Indicative Mood we say, "I *love*," "Thou *lovest*," "He *loves*;" but in the Subjunctive we should say, "(If) I *love*," "(If) thou *love*," "(If) he *love*." **Wert**, which occurs in the Past Subjunctive of the Verb "TO BE," **is the only word in the language *peculiar* to this Mood.**

The Subjunctive follows the Conjunctions **if, though, although, lest,** &c. "**If**" may be understood; as "*Were I*" = "*If I were.*"

See §§ 232 to 234 inclusive, also the Paradigms.

191. The **Potential** Mood implies **power, liberty, necessity, wish,** or **duty**; as, "I *can go*" = "I am able to go;" "I *may go*" = "I am at liberty to go;" "I *must go*" = "I am under a necessity to go." '*May go,*' '*can go,*' and '*must go*' are in the Potential Mood.

The Potential is a **Compound** Mood formed by the aid of Auxiliary Verbs. Learn this:—

> The **Auxiliary signs** of Potential Mood,
> Are may, can, must, might, could, would, and should.

See §§ 230, 231, and the Paradigms.

Exercise 21.

Tell the **Mood** of each of the Finite Verbs which occur in the following sentences:—

The children in Iceland are educated at home. Ring out the old year. Be warned by this, lest worse befall you. Water is the natural drink of mankind. All men must die. If John go, you should stay at home. Haste to the ferry. I came from Acton, whence came ye? Have you ever tasted this water? The pupils may now be dismissed. The seamen harpooned a whale, which they could not secure. A whale can shatter a boat with one blow. Let well enough alone. We should learn our lessons. The master may require you. Tim looked up. Come hither, my little page. John might compete if he were two years older. God save the Queen. Oh, kill that great ugly spider that is running across the floor! Stay! Do you know what a piece of mechanism that creature is? I hardly think you do, or you would neither call it ugly nor crush it out of shape. I would be like an angel. John should have obeyed his father. Green be thy fields.

MEANING OF THE TERMS FINITE AND INFINITE AS APPLIED TO VERBS.

192. When a Verb is used with a Subject or Nominative it is said to be **Finite**, which means *limited* or *restricted*. Thus, when I say "John reads," the reading is limited or restricted to *John*, the SUBJECT. The four *preceding Moods* make up the **FINITE VERB**. When a *Verb is used* without a Subject it is said to be **Infinite**, which means *unlimited* (that is, by a Subject); as, "He came *to be amused;*" "*To learn* is profitable." "*To be amused*" and "*to learn*" have no Subject. The **Verb Infinite** includes the Infinitive Mood (proper), and the Participles.

193. The **Infinitive Mood** is that form of the Verb which is preceded by the word '**to**;' as, *to work, to be singing, to be praised, to have been praised.* '*To*' is understood after the Verbs **bid, dare, need, feel, hear, let, make, see,** and the Auxiliaries **shall, will, may, can, must, do**; as, "I saw him (to) come," "I heard her (to) sing," "Bid him (to) sit down," "Let the prisoner (to) go," "You must not (to) do it."

USES OF THE INFINITIVE.

194. The Infinitive Mood is used—

(*a*) As an **Abstract Noun**; *e.g.*, "I like *to learn*"="I like *learning.*" "*To talk* is forbidden" = "*Talking* is forbidden."

(*b*) To express a **Purpose**; as, "I went *to see* him"="I went *for the purpose of* seeing him." "I came *to be instructed*" = "I came *for the purpose of* being instructed."

(*c*) **After a Noun** or **Pronoun**, as part of a group of words forming the Direct Object of a Transitive Verb; as, "I ordered *James to be sent;*" "I believe *John to be an honest man.*" Here the full Direct Object of '*ordered*' is 'James to be sent,' as you may see by asking, 'I ordered what?' Ans. '*James to be sent,*' not '*James.*' Similarly the Direct Object of '*believe*' is '*John to be an honest man,*' for that is *what* I believe. Notice that 'James *to be sent*' = '*that* James *should be sent,*' and 'John *to be* an honest man' = *that* John *is* an honest man.' See § 296.

(*d*) **To describe Nouns**; as, A farm *to sell* or *to be sold;* Chairs *to mend* or *to be mended;* A house *to let* or *to be let;* An axe *to grind.*

When the Infinitive is thus used, it may be converted *into an Abstract* Noun governed by *for*; as, A house to *let* = A house *for letting;* Bread *to sell* = Bread *for selling,* or *for sale.*

195. Learn the following **six forms** which the Infinitive of a Transitive Verb assumes :—

TRANSITIVE VERB—TO WRITE.

INFINITIVE MOOD.

	ACTIVE VOICE.	PASSIVE VOICE.
Present Indef.	**To write.**	**To be written.**
,, *Prog.*	**To be writing.**	(None.)
Past Perfect.	**To have written.**	**To have been written.**
Perfect Prog.	**To have been writing.**	(None.)

PARTICIPLES AND THEIR USES.

196. Participles participate in the nature of Verbs and Adjectives; for, whilst implying *action* as Verbs, like Adjectives they *refer to Nouns.* Thus we speak of '*stars twinkling,*' 'money *earned,*' 'ships *having sailed,*' 'crews *having been lost.*' See also §§. 98 and 201.

197. Verbs have **two Simple** Participles—a **Present** ending in **ing**, as, *singing;* and a **Past** ending in various ways, but generally in **d, t,** and **en,** as, *loved, heard, meant, smitten.* The Simple Present Participle of Verbs implying action, is of the **Active** Voice; because (1) the Noun to which it refers *denotes* the **doer** of the action, and (2) it takes a **Direct Object** after it when it is Transitive; as, "I like to hear Jane *singing* a *song.*" Here the Present
Doer. Part. Dir. Obj.
Participle '*singing*' refers to '*Jane,*' the doer, and '*song*' is its Direct Object.

The Simple Past Participle is **Passive**; for the action it denotes is **done to** the person or thing named by the Noun to which it refers; as, "I heard the *song sung* by Jane." Here the Participle '*sung*' refers to '*song,*' and denotes an action *done to* the song, therefore it is Passive.

198. Verbs have **three Compound** Participles :—

(1.) The **Compound Present,** formed by putting '*being*' before the Past Participle; as, '*(being) sung.*' This Participle is **Passive,** for we speak of the song *being sung,* that is, of something being *done* to the song.

(2.) **The Compound Past Participle** of the **Active Voice,** formed by putting '*having*' before the Past Participle; as, '(*having*) *sung*.' This Participle is Active, for the Noun to which it refers denotes the doer of the action, and when Transitive it takes a Direct Object; as, "Jane *having sung* a *song*, left the room."

(3.) **The Compound Past Participle** of the **Passive Voice,** formed by putting '*having been*' before the Past Participle; as, '(*having been*) *sung*.' '*Having been sung*' is **Passive,** for we speak of a song *having been sung,* which means something **done to** the song.

199. Learn the following **five forms** which the Participles of a Transitive Verb assume:—

VERB TO WRITE.

PARTICIPLES.

ACTIVE VOICE.	PASSIVE VOICE.
Simple Present. **Writing.**	*Comp. Present.* **Being written.**
Simple Past. (None.)	*Simple Past.* **Written.**
Comp. Past. **Having written.**	*Comp. Past.* **Having been written.**

200. The two Simple Participles may be used—

(*a*) Purely as **Adjectives**; *e.g.*, "the *setting* sun," "a *wounded* soldier." Parse '*setting*' and '*wounded*' as 'Participles used as Adjectives.'

(*b*) As **Parts of Stating Verbs**; *e.g.*, "The sun *is* (*setting*)," "The tide *has* (*ebbed*)." Parse '*is setting*' and '*has ebbed*' as Verbs; and don't separate '*is*' and '*setting*,' '*has*' and '*ebbed*;' for the two words, in each case, are needed to make the statement.

201. The **Present Participle** is often used as a **Noun.** Parse '*swimming*' and '*doing*' **Verbal Nouns** in "*Swimming* is healthful." "There is joy in *doing* good." The Verbal Noun in **ing** is called the **Gerund.**

202. Read carefully the following sentences which illustrate some of the **uses of true Participles,** as distinguished from Participial Adjectives and Verbal Nouns:—"The monkeys *kept* at the gardens are amusing" (Participle '*kept*' = '**which are kept**'). "*Driving* along the street

I met Frank" ('driving' = 'when I was driving'). "I heard the thunder *rolling*" ('rolling' = 'that it was rolling'). "*Having finished* my work I returned" ('having finished' = 'when I had finished'). "The boy *having been praised* too much, grew vain" ('having been praised' = 'because he had been praised').

Now you will understand that the proper use of Participles, as such, is to **express briefly** what would otherwise require a **Relative Pronoun** and a **Stating Verb**; or a **Conjunction**, a **Pronoun**, and a **Stating Verb**.

Exercise 22.

(*a.*) Name the following Infinitive forms:—

To hurt, to have been sent, to be going, to have, to have been, to have been teaching, to learn, to be learning, to have learned, to have been killed, to be cut, to be eating, to have been eaten, to do, to be doing, to be done, to have seen.

(*b.*) Name the following Participial forms:—

Sending, having sent, having been injured, rowing, being shown, having heard, being done, finishing, finished, having finished, being finished, gone, going, having gone, being smitten, smiting, having smitten, having been smitten, being sent.

(*c.*) Write out, or tell orally, all the Infinitive forms of the six following Verbs: Take, make, shake, smite, love, give.

(*d.*) Write out, or tell orally, all the Participial forms of the same six Verbs.

VOICE.

203. That form of a Transitive Verb which shows whether the Subject **does** the action, or the action is **done** to the Subject, is called **Voice**. (See §§ 93 and 94).

Transitive Verbs have two voices—

The **Active**; as, the dog *bites*; and

The **Passive**; as, the dog *is bitten*.

204. The Passive Voice is formed by putting the *several Moods* and Tenses of the Verb 'To Be' before the *Past Participle* of a Transitive Verb, in this way—

	Active Voice.	**Passive Voice.**
Present Tense.	I love.	I (*am*) loved.
Past ,,	I loved.	I (*was*) loved.
Future ,,	I shall love.	I (*shall be*) loved.
Fut. Perf. ,,	I shall have loved.	I (*shall have been*) loved.
Pres. Perf. ,,	I have loved.	I (*have been*) loved.
Past Perf. ,,	I had loved.	I (*had been*) loved.
Present Infinitive.	To love.	(*To be*) loved.
Past ,,	To have loved.	(*To have been*) loved.
Present Participle.	Loving.	(*Being*) loved.
Compound Past Participle.	Having loved.	(*Having been*) loved.

* The Verb 'To Be' is called the **Voice** Auxiliary: it has eleven simple forms—**be, been, being, is, was, wast, am, are, art, were,** and **wert**. See the Paradigm of the Passive Voice of the Verb 'To Call.'

MEANING OF STRONG, WEAK, REGULAR, IRREGULAR, AND DEFECTIVE VERBS.

205. A **Strong** Verb adds nothing to the Present Tense to form the Past, but simply changes the vowel of the Present; as, 'I sm*i*te,' 'I sm*o*te;' 'I f*a*ll,' 'I f*e*ll.'

Notice that **i** is changed to **o** and **a** to **e** in the above examples, and that nothing is added.

206. A **Weak** Verb is one that adds **ed, d,** or **t** to the Present Tense to form the Past, accompanied in some cases by *change* or *shortening* of the vowel in the Present; as, 'I call,' 'I call*ed*;' 'I love,' 'I lov*ed*;' 'I sleep,' 'I slep*t*;' 'I sell,' 'I s*o*ld;' 'I bleed,' I bled.'

Notice that '*bleed*' only shortens the vowel to form '*bled*,' which is, nevertheless, a contracted form of '*bleeded*.'

207. A **Regular** Verb forms its Past Tense and Past Participle by adding **d** or **ed** to the Present Tense; as,

Present,	Roll.	*Past*,	Rolled.	*Past Part.*,	Rolled.
,,	Love.	,,	Loved..	,, ,,	Loved.

208. An **Irregular** Verb does **not** form its Past Tense and Past Participle by adding **d** or **ed** to the Present Tense; as,

Present,	Blow.	*Past*,	Blew.	*Past Part.*,	Blown.
	Sell.	,,	Sold.	,, ,,	Sold.
	Hit.	,,	Hit.	,, ,,	Hit.

209. **Defective** Verbs want some of their parts, such as the Infinitive Mood, the Participles, &c. They are **shall, will, may, can, must, forego,** and **beware.**

'**Ought**' is sometimes classed with the Defective Verbs; but it is a form of the Past Tense of the Verb 'OWE,' which is not Defective. **Beware** is mostly used in the Imperative Mood; as,

> **Beware the pine tree's withered branch!**
> **Beware the awful avalanche.**

CLASSIFIED LIST OF IRREGULAR VERBS.

FIRST CLASS.

210. **Those which have *one form* for the three parts:**

Present.	*Past.*	*Past Part.*
(*I*) Burst	(*I*) burst	(*I have*) burst
„ Cast	„ cast	„ cast
„ Cost	„ cost	„ cost
„ Cut	„ cut	„ cut

The remaining Verbs of this class are—*hit, hurt, let, put, rid, set, shed, shut, slit, split, spread, sweat, thrust.*

SECOND CLASS.

Those which have *two distinct forms* for the three parts.

NOTE.—Those with the letter *r* prefixed are also *Regular*.

Present.	*Past.*	*Past Participle.*
(*I*) Abide	(*I*) abode	(*I have*) abode
„ Beat	„ beat	„ beaten
„ Behold	„ beheld	„ beheld
„ *r*Bend	„ bent	„ bent
„ *r*Bereave	„ bereft	„ bereft
„ Beseech	„ besought	„ besought
„ Bind	„ bound	„ bound
„ Bleed	„ bled	„ bled
„ *Breed*	„ bred	„ bred
„ *Bring*	„ brought	„ brought
„ *rBuild*	„ built	„ built

Present.	*Past.*	*Past Participle.*
(*I*) *r* Burn	(*I*) burnt	(*I have*) burnt
„ Buy	„ bought	„ bought
„ Catch	„ caught	„ caught
„ Cling	„ clung	„ clung
„ Come	„ came	„ come
„ Creep	„ crept	„ crept
„ *r* Deal	„ dealt	„ dealt
„ *r* Dig	„ dug	„ dug
„ *r* Dream	„ dreamt	„ dreamt
„ Dwell	„ dwelt	„ dwelt
„ Feed	„ fed	„ fed
„ Feel	„ felt	„ felt
„ Fight	„ fought	„ fought
„ Find	„ found	„ found
„ Flee	„ fled	„ fled
„ Fling	„ flung	„ flung
„ Get	„ got	„ got
„ *r* Gild	„ gilt	„ gilt
„ *r* Gird	„ girt	„ girt
„ Grind	„ ground	„ ground
„ *r* Hang *	„ hung	„ hung
„ Have	„ had	„ had
„ Hold	„ held	„ held
„ Keep	„ kept	„ kept
„ *r* Kneel	„ knelt	„ knelt
„ Lead	„ led	„ led
„ Leave	„ left	„ left
„ Lend	„ lent	„ lent
„ Lose	„ lost	„ lost
„ Make	„ made	„ made
„ Mean	„ meant	„ meant
„ Meet	„ met	„ met
„ Rĕad	„ rĕad	„ rĕad
„ Rend	„ rent	„ rent
„ Run	„ ran	„ run
„ Seek	„ sought	„ sought
„ Sell	„ sold	„ sold
„ Send	„ sent	„ sent
„ *r* Shine	„ shone	„ shone
„ Shoe	„ shod	„ shod

* *Hang*, to take away life, is regular; as, "The man has been *hanged*."

Present.	*Past.*	*Past Participle.*
(*I*) Shoot	(*I*) shot	(*I have*) shot
" Sit	" sat	" sat
" Sleep	" slept	" slept
" Sling	" slung	" slung
" *r* Smell	" smelt	" smelt
" Speed	" sped	" sped
" Spend	" spent	" spent
" Spill	" spilt	" spilt
" Stand	" stood	" stood
" Sting	" stung	" stung
" Strike	" struck	" struck *or* stricken
" String	" strung	" strung
" Sweep	" swept	" swept
" Swing	" swung	" swung
" Teach	" taught	" taught
" Tell	" told	" told
" Think	" thought	" thought
" Weep	" wept	" wept
" Win	" won	" won
" Wind	" wound	" wound
" *r* Work	" wrought	" wrought
" Wring	" wrung	" wrung

THIRD CLASS.

Those which have *three distinct forms* for the three parts.

Present.	*Past.*	*Past Participle.*
(*I*) Arise	(*I*) arose	(*I have*) arisen
" Bear, *to carry*	" bore *or* bare	" borne
" Bear, *to bring forth*	" bore *or* bare	" born
" Begin	" began	" begun
" Bid	" bid *or* bade	" bidden
" Bite	" bit	" bitten *or* bit
" Blow	" blew	" blown
" Break	" broke	" broken
" Chide	" chid	" chidden
" *Choose*	" chose	" chosen
" *Cleave, to split*	" cleft or clove	" cleft or cloven

Present.	*Past.*	*Past Participle.*
(*I*) *r*Clothe	(*I*) clothed	(*I have*) clad
„ *r*Dare	„ durst	„ dared
„ Do	„ did	„ done
„ Draw	„ drew	„ drawn
„ Drink	„ drank	„ drunk
„ Drive	„ drove	„ driven
„ Eat	„ ate	„ eaten
„ Fall	„ fell	„ fallen
„ Fly	„ flew	„ flown
„ Forsake	„ forsook	„ forsaken
„ Freeze	„ froze	„ frozen
„ Give	„ gave	„ given
„ *r*Grave	„ graved	„ graven
„ Grow	„ grew	„ grown
„ *r*Hew	„ hewed	„ hewn
„ Hide	„ hid	„ hidden
„ Know	„ knew	„ known
„ *r*Lade	„ laded	„ laden
„ Lie	„ lay	„ lain
„ *r*Mow	„ mowed	„ mown
„ Ride	„ rode	„ ridden
„ Ring	„ rang	„ rung
„ Rise	„ rose	„ risen
„ Rive	„ rived	„ riven
„ See	„ saw	„ seen
„ Sew	„ sewed	„ sewn
„ Shake	„ shook	„ shaken
„ *r*Shave	„ shaved	„ shaven
„ *r*Shear	„ shore	„ shorn
„ *r*Show	„ showed	„ shown
„ Shrink	„ shrank	„ shrunk
„ Sing	„ sang	„ sung
„ Sink	„ sank	„ sunk
„ Slay	„ slew	„ slain
„ *r*Slide	„ slid	„ slidden
„ Slink	„ slank	„ slunk
„ Smite	„ smote	„ smitten
„ *r*Sow	„ sowed	„ sown
„ Speak	„ spoke	„ spoken
„ Spin	„ span	„ spun
„ Spit	„ spat	„ spit
„ Spring	„ sprang	„ sprung

Present.	*Past.*	*Past Participle.*
(*I*) Steal	(*I*) stole	(*I have*) stolen
" Stride	" strode	" stridden
" Strive	" strove	" striven
" *r*Strew *or* }	" strewed *or* }	" strewn *or*
" *r*Strow }	" strowed }	" strown
" Swear	" swore	" sworn
" *r*Swell	" swelled	" swollen
" Swim	" swam	" swum
" Take	" took	" taken
" Tear	" tore	" torn
" Thrive	" throve	" thriven
" Throw	" threw	" thrown
" Tread	" trod	" trodden
" *r*Wax	" waxed	" waxen
" Wear	" wore	" worn
" Weave	" wove	" woven
" Write	" wrote	" written

211. You should learn the above list of Verbs thoroughly, as mistakes are liable to be made, such as using the Past Tense for the Past Participle, and the Past Participle for the Past Tense. Read them aloud again and again, always putting '*I*' before the Present and the Past, and '*I have*' before the Past Participle, thus :—'I *sing*,' 'I *sang*,' 'I have *sung*.' Past Participle '*sung*.'

CONJUGATION.*

212. The **simple** Conjugation of a Verb is the *putting together* of its simple forms as they occur in its simple Moods and Tenses. When all the simple and compound forms needed to express the changes of Voice, Mood, Tense, Number, and Person are put together in order, a Verb is said to be **fully conjugated.**

213. English Verbs have very **few endings** (Inflections), and hence great use is made of **Auxiliary Verbs** in expressing Voice, Mood, and Tense. The Auxiliaries

---

* **Lat.** *conjugatus* = put together.

are **Be (Am), Do, Have, Shall, Will, May, Can, Must.** Be, Do, Will, and Have are used also as Principal Verbs.

214. Auxiliaries are classed as—

(*a*) **Tense** Auxiliaries—Shall, Will, Have, Do, Be.
(*b*) A **Voice** Auxiliary—Be.
(*c*) **Mood** Auxiliaries—May, Can, Must, Might, Could, Would, Should.

215. '**Be**' may be used before either the *Present* or the *Past* Participle; as, 'I am *calling*,' 'I am *called*.' '**Have**' and its Past Tense '**Had**' can only be used before the *Past* Participle; as, 'I have *called*,' 'I had *written*.'

> **Shall, Will, May, Can, Must,** and **Do,**
> Are followed by the Infinitive Mood wanting sign '*to*.'

USES OF THE AUXILIARY VERBS.

'TO BE.'

216. 'To Be' is used in forming the **Progressive Tenses** and the **Passive Voice.**

217. A **Progressive Tense** is formed by putting the *Present* Participle of another Verb after a Tense of the Verb 'To Be' thus: 'I *am (running)*.' 'I *was (reading)*.' 'I *shall be (writing)*.' 'I *have been (singing)*.' The above forms are Active; but 'I *am (being called)*,' 'I *was (being called)*,' are Progressive Tenses of the Passive Voice. See Paradigm of 'To Call.'

218. The **Passive Voice** is formed by putting the various Moods and Tenses of the Verb 'To Be' before the *Past* Participle of a **Transitive** Verb. See Paradigm of the Verb 'To Call,' Passive Voice; also § 204.

219. By using the Present Tense of the Verb 'To Be' before the Past Participle of *Verbs implying motion*, we obtain a form of the *Present Perfect Tense* of such Verbs; as, "He *is come*" = "He *has come*." "The ship *is arrived*" = "The ship *has arrived*." "John *is gone*." "The bird *is flown*." The Past Tense of the Verb 'To Be' is also

sometimes used before the Past Participles of Verbs of motion, to form the Past Perfect Tense; as, "Thy mother from thy side for evermore *was gone*." 'To Be,' in such cases, is purely a **Tense Auxiliary**.

'TO DO.'

220. The Auxiliary Verb 'To Do' is used both to express **emphasis** and to **ask questions**.

221. Verbs are conjugated **emphatically** by laying the stress of the voice on '*Do*' or '*Did*' placed before their Infinitive Mood, the sign '*to*' being suppressed; thus—

INDICATIVE MOOD.

Emphatic Present Tense.

Singular.	*Plural.*
1. *I* **do work.**	1. *We* **do work.**
2. *Thou* **dost work.**	2. *You* **do work.**
3. *He* **does work.**	3. *They* **do work.**

Negative form—*I* **do not work**, &c.

Emphatic Past Tense.

Singular.	*Plural.*
1. *I* **did work.**	1. *We* **did work.**
2. *Thou* **didst work.**	2. *You* **did work.**
3. *He* **did work.**	3. *They* **did work.**

Negative form—*I* **did not work**, &c.

222. When the stress of the voice is not laid on 'Do' and 'Did' the above are not emphatic, but **expletive** forms of the Present Tense and the Past: 'I do love' = 'I love;' 'I did love' = 'I loved.' The word '*expletive*' means '**filling out.**' These forms are sometimes used in poetry to fill out or complete the number of syllables needed in a line, hence the name '*expletive;*' *e.g.*—

"I am a linen-draper bold,
As all the world *doth know*."

"The wind *did blow*, the cloak *did fly*,
Like streamer long and gay."

INTERROGATIVE CONJUGATION.

223. The following examples will illustrate the use of '**Do**' as an **Interrogative** Auxiliary :—

INDICATIVE MOOD—PRESENT TENSE.

Singular.	*Plural.*
1. **Do** *I* **sing?**	1. **Do** *we* **sing?**
2. **Dost** *thou* **sing?**	2. **Do** *you* **sing?**
3. **Does** *he* **sing?**	3. **Do** *they* **sing?**

INDICATIVE MOOD—PAST TENSE.

Singular.	*Plural.*
1. **Did** *I* **sing?**	1. **Did** *we* **sing?**
2. **Didst** *thou* **sing?**	2. **Did** *you* **sing?**
3. **Did** *he* **sing?**	3. **Did** *they* **sing?**

224. The foregoing is equivalent to the following SIMPLE INTERROGATIVE CONJUGATION :—

PRESENT TENSE.

Singular.	*Plural.*
1. **Sing** *I?*	1. **Sing** *we?*
2. **Singest** *thou?*	2. **Sing** *you?*
3. **Sings** *he?*	3. **Sing** *they?*

PAST TENSE.

Singular.	*Plural.*
1. **Sang** *I?*	1. **Sang** *we?*
2. **Sangest** *thou?*	2. **Sang** *you?*
3. **Sang** *he?*	3. **Sang** *they?*

This simple mode of conjugating Principal Verbs (with the exception of **Be** and **Have**) is now seldom used.

'TO HAVE.'

225. The Tenses of the Verb 'To HAVE' are used before the *Past Participle* of other Verbs to form their **Perfect Tenses**, thus—

I **have** *spoken* (**Present** Perfect Tense).
I **had** *spoken* (**Past** Perfect Tense).
I **shall have** *spoken* (**Future** Perfect Tense).

SHALL AND WILL.

226. Some of the uses of SHALL and WILL, as the *Auxiliaries* of the Future Tense, are mentioned at § 184;

but what is there said refers to **Direct Statements.** Thus, in Direct Statements, SHALL in the *First* Person, and WILL in the *Second* and *Third* denote **simple** futurity; whilst WILL in the *First* Person, and SHALL in the *Second* and *Third*, are **emphatic**, indicating purpose, duty, obligation, &c.; *e.g.*—

Simple Future.	Emphatic Future.
I *shall go* to town.	I *will go* to town.
You *will go* to town.	You *shall go* to town.
He *will go* to town.	He *shall go* to town.

227. Learn the following:—

When the Future Tense is used **Indirectly** in the Second or Third Person, Shall or Will may be either emphatic or unemphatic, according to the sense we wish to convey; *e.g.*:

Simple Future.	Emphatic Future.
You think you *shall succeed.*	You say you *will go.*
John says he *shall die.*	John says he *will go.*
John says you *will go.*	John says you *shall go.*
You say John *will go.*	You say John *shall go.*

In "John says he *shall die*," "*shall die*" is evidently a *simple* Future, for John's words when quoted directly are, "*I shall die*" (expressing *mere futurity*). In the same manner you may show that "*will go*" in "John says he *will go*" is *emphatic*, because John's words when directly quoted are *emphatic*, viz., "I *will go*." The rest may be similarly explained.

228. When the Future Tense is used **Interrogatively**, you should almost always put SHALL before '*I*' or '*we*;' as, *Shall* I go? *Shall* we go? WILL, however, might be used interrogatively in the *First* Person, if I were asking another either to determine my will, or to express an opinion as to what I intend; as, "Which *will* I choose?" "What move *will* I make?"

Learn the following simple rules regarding the **Interrogative** use of SHALL and WILL in the **Second** and **Third** Persons:—

1. Use SHALL to ask a question in either the *Second Person or the Third*, when you may expect SHALL in the *answer*; as, "*Shall* you be elected?"; Answer expected—

"I hope I *shall*," not "I hope I *will*;" or "I fear I *shall* not," not "I fear I *will* not."

2. Use WILL to ask a question in either the *Second* Person or the *Third*, if you may expect WILL in the **answer**; as, "*Will* you come to-day?" Answer expected—"I *will*, or I *will not*." "*Will* your friend call to-morrow?" Answer expected—"He *will*, or he *will not*."

But notice that a request made with WILL may be answered in SHALL; *e.g.*, "*Will* you dine with me to-morrow?" Ans. "I *shall* be happy to do so." The reply, however, might be simply "I *will* do so."

NOTE.—As a general rule, **Will** expresses the *will* or *pleasure* of its own Subject; whilst **Shall** denotes that the *will* of its Subject is subordinated to that of some one else, or to some external circumstance.

MAY, CAN, AND MUST.

229. These Verbs, together with SHOULD and WOULD, are classed as the Auxiliaries of the **Potential Mood**. **May** denotes liberty, **Can** denotes power, **Must** denotes necessity.

230. The **POTENTIAL MOOD has four** Tenses:—

1. The **Present Tense**, formed by putting *May*, *Can*, or *Must* before the *Infinitive* of another Verb, with the sign '*to*' omitted; as,

I *may*, *can*, or *must write*,
Thou *mayst*, *canst*, or *must write*, &c.

2. The **Past Tense**, formed by putting *Might*, *Could*, *Would*, or *Should* before the *Infinitive* of another Verb with the sign *to* omitted; as, I *might*, *could*, *would*, or *should write*, &c.

3. The **Present Perfect Tense**, formed by putting *May have*, *Can have*, or *Must have* before the *Past Participle* of another Verb; as, I *may have*, *can have*, or *must have written*, &c.

4. The **Past Perfect Tense**, formed by putting *Might have*, *Could have*, *Would have*, or *Should have* before the

Past Participle of another Verb; as, I *might have, coud have, would have,* or *should have written,* &c. See Paradigm of the Verb 'To Call,' Potential Mood.

231. In the Present Potential, 'MAY' and 'MUST' generally refer to the **future**; whilst 'CAN' usually denotes present time. Observe likewise that the Past Potential is a Past Tense only in **form** and **name**; for it indicates either **future** or **present** time.

'MAY' and 'CAN' are **Present Tense forms**; and 'MIGHT,' 'COULD,' 'WOULD,' and 'SHOULD,' **Past Tense forms.**

THE TENSES OF THE SUBJUNCTIVE.

232. Only **three** Tenses of the Conditional or Subjunctive Mood are given in the Paradigms of the Verbs 'To BE,' and 'To CALL,' viz.—the **Present**, the **Past**, and the **Present Perfect**. Some forms characteristic of the Subjunctive, are found in each of these, when the **full** conjugation is stated; but in the remaining Tenses, there is nothing to distinguish this Mood from the Indicative. The tendency is, and has been for a long time, to do away with the forms characteristic of the Subjunctive.

233. What is called the **Present Tense** of the Subjunctive is really a **contingent Future**, with the form of a Present; *e.g.*, "If it *rain* to-morrow, John won't go to town." Here, "if it *rain*" evidently refers to the future. The **proper use** of the Present Subjunctive is to express a contingent future action or event. In the sentence, "Look if it *rains*," the **Indicative Mood** is **properly used**; for the meaning is, "Look if it is now actually raining."

Instead of the simple Present Subjunctive, we may use a compound form which has the same meaning. For example, we may say either—

'If I *go*,' or 'If I *should go*.'
'If thou *go*,' or 'If thou *shouldst go*.'
'If he *go*,' or 'If he *should go*.'
'If we *go*,' or 'If we *should go*.'
'If you *go*,' or 'If you should go.'
'If they *go*,' or 'If they should go.'

Notice in regard to this equivalent form—

1. That the Auxiliary '*should*' does not change to '*would*' in the Second and Third Persons;
2. That in the Second Person, Singular, '*shouldst*' and not '*should*' is used; and
3. That '*should*' does not here denote *duty*.

Distinguish this *compound* Tense of the Subjunctive, from the Past Potential of the same form, denoting *duty; e.g.*, "Children *should obey* their parents."

234. What is called the **Past Tense** of the Subjunctive is *usually* **a contingent Present**; *e.g.*, "If I *were* John, I would act differently," that is, "If I [at the present time] were John, &c.;" "If he *were asked* he would go," which may mean, "If he were [now] asked he would go."

SIMPLE CONJUGATION—EXAMPLES.

235. THE VERB **DO** [PRINCIPAL AND AUXILIARY.]

INDICATIVE MOOD.

PRESENT TENSE.

Singular.	*Plural.*
1. *I* do.	1. *We* do.
2. *Thou* doest or dost.	2. *You* do.
3. *He* does or doth.	3. *They* do.

PAST TENSE.

Singular.	*Plural.*
1. *I* did.	1. *We* did.
2. *Thou* didst.	2. *You* did.
3. *He* did.	3. *They* did.

SUBJUNCTIVE MOOD.

PRESENT TENSE.

Singular.	*Plural.*
1. (If) *I* do.	1. (If) *we* do.
2. (If) *thou* do.	2. (If) *you* do.
3. (If) *he* do.	3. (If) *they* do.

IMPERATIVE MOOD.

2. **Do** (*thou.*)	2. **Do** (*you.*)

INFINITIVE MOOD.

To do.

PARTICIPLES.

PRES. **Doing.**	PAST. **Done.**

236. THE VERB **HAVE** [PRINCIPAL AND AUXILIARY.]

INDICATIVE MOOD.

PRESENT TENSE.

Singular.	*Plural.*
1. *I* **have.**	1. *We* **have.**
2. *Thou* **hast.**	2. *You* **have.**
3. *He* **has** or **hath.**	3. *They* **have.**

PAST TENSE.

Singular.	*Plural.*
1. *I* **had.**	1. *We* **had.**
2. *Thou* **hadst.**	2. *You* **had.**
3. *He* **had.**	3. *They* **had.**

SUBJUNCTIVE MOOD.

PRESENT TENSE.

Singular.	*Plural.*
1. (If) *I* **have.**	1. (If) *we* **have.**
2. (If) *thou* **have.**	2. (If) *you* **have.**
3. (If) *he* **have.**	3. (If) *they* **have.**

IMPERATIVE MOOD.

2. **Have** (*thou.*)	2. **Have** (*you.*)

INFINITIVE MOOD.

To have.

PARTICIPLES.

PRES. **Having.**	PAST. **Had.**

237. THE VERB **SHALL** [AUXILIARY.]

INDICATIVE MOOD.

PRESENT TENSE.

Singular.	*Plural.*
1. *I* **shall.**	1. *We* **shall.**
2. *Thou* **shalt.**	2. *You* **shall.**
3. *He* **shall.**	3. *They* **shall.**

PAST TENSE.

Singular.	*Plural.*
1. *I* should.	1. *We* should.
2. *Thou* shouldst.	2. *You* should.
3. *He* should.	3. *They* should.

INFINITIVE MOOD.
(*Wanting.*)

PARTICIPLES.
(*Wanting.*)

38. THE VERB WILL [AUXILIARY.]

INDICATIVE MOOD.

PRESENT TENSE.

Singular.	*Plural.*
1. *I* will.	1. *We* will.
2. *Thou* wilt.	2. *You* will.
3. *He* will.	3. *They* will.

PAST TENSE.

Singular.	*Plural.*
1. *I* would.	1. *We* would.
2. *Thou* wouldst.	2. *You* would.
3. *He* would.	3. *They* would.

INFINITIVE MOOD.
(*Wanting.*)

PARTICIPLES.
(*Wanting.*)

[WILL, when it signifies 'to bequeath,' 'to desire,' &c., is a Regular, Transitive Verb, having all its parts. Thus—

Present, *Will*. Past, *Willed*. Past Part., *Willed*.
Present Part., *Willing*. Infinitive, *To Will*.

Examples—"The father *willed* his estate to his son." "Father, I *will* that they also whom thou hast given me be with me where I am." (John xvii. 24.)]

239. THE VERB MAY [AUXILIARY.]

INDICATIVE MOOD.

PRESENT TENSE.

Singular.	*Plural.*
1. *I* may.	1. *We* may.
2. *Thou* mayest.	2. *You* may.
3. *He* may.	3. *They* may.

PAST TENSE.

Singular.	*Plural.*
1. *I* might.	1. *We* might.
2. *Thou* mightst.	2. *You* might.
3. *He* might.	3. *They* might.

INFINITIVE MOOD.
(*Wanting.*)

PARTICIPLES.
(*Wanting.*)

240. THE VERB CAN [AUXILIARY.]

INDICATIVE MOOD.

PRESENT TENSE.

Singular.	*Plural.*
1. *I* can.	1. *We* can.
2. *Thou* canst.	2. *You* can.
3. *He* can.	3. *They* can.

PAST TENSE.

Singular.	*Plural.*
1. *I* could.	1. *We* could.
2. *Thou* couldst.	2. *You* could.
3. *He* could.	3. *They* could.

INFINITIVE MOOD.
(*Wanting.*)

PARTICIPLES.
(*Wanting.*)

241. THE VERB MUST [AUXILIARY.]

INDICATIVE MOOD.

PRESENT AND PAST TENSE.

Singular.	*Plural.*
1. *I* must.	1. *We* must.
2. *Thou* must.	2. *You* must.
3. *He* must.	3. *They* must.

NOTE.—This is the simplest Verb in the English language: it has no variation.

DARE and OWE.—These Verbs are peculiar. Thus, in the Present Tense of DARE, we may say either 'he *dare*' or 'he *dares*,' and the Past has two forms with different meanings—'I *durst*'='I *am allowed*,' and 'I *dared*'='I *challenged*.' **Durst** has no variation. OWE has two forms of the Past—'I *ought*'='I *should*,' and 'I *owed*'='I *was indebted to*.' **Ought** has one variation, 'thou *oughtest*.'

FULL CONJUGATION.

242. THE VERB BE [PRINCIPAL AND AUXILIARY.]

INDICATIVE MOOD.

PRESENT TENSE.

	Singular.	*Plural.*
INDEFINITE	1. *I* am.	1. *We* are.
	2. *Thou* art.	2. *You* are.
	3. *He* is.	3. *They* are.

PAST TENSE.

	Singular.	*Plural.*
INDEFINITE	1. *I* was.	1. *We* were.
	2. *Thou* wast.	2. *You* were.
	3. *He* was.	3. *They* were.

FUTURE TENSE.

	Singular.	*Plural.*
INDEFINITE	1. *I* shall be.	1. *We* shall be.
	2. *Thou* wilt be.	2. You will be.
	3. *He* will be.	3. They will be.

Present Perfect.

Singular.	Plural.
1. *I* have been.	1. *We* have been.
2. *Thou* hast been.	2. *You* have been.
3. *He* has been.	3. *They* have been.

Past Perfect.

Singular.	Plural.
1. *I* had been.	1. *We* had been.
2. *Thou* hadst been.	2. *You* had been.
3. *He* had been.	3. *They* had been.

Future Perfect.

Singular.	Plural.
1. *I* shall have been.	1. *We* shall have been.
2. *Thou* wilt have been.	2. *You* will have been.
3. *He* will have been.	3. *They* will have been.

SUBJUNCTIVE MOOD.

Present Tense.

	Singular.	Plural.
Indefinite	1. (If) *I* be.	1. (If) *we* be.
	2. (If) *thou* be.	2. (If) *you* be.
	3. (If) *he* be.	3. (If) *they* be.

Compound Form.—(If) *I* should be; (If) *thou* shouldst be; (If) *he* should be, &c.

Past Tense.

	Singular.	Plural.
Indefinite	1. (If) *I* were.	1. (If) *we* were.
	2. (If) *thou* wert.	2. (If) *you* were.
	3. (If) *he* were.	3. (If) *they* were.

Present Perfect.

Singular.	Plural.
1. (If) *I* have been.	1. (If) *we* have been.
2. (If) *thou* have been.	2. (If) *you* have been.
3. (If) *he* have been.	3. (If) *they* have been.

POTENTIAL MOOD.

Present Tense.

	Singular.	Plural.
Indefinite	1. *I* may, can, or must be.	1. *We* may, can, or must be.
	2. *Thou* mayst, canst, or must be.	2. *You* may, can, or must be.
	3. *He* may, can, or must be.	3. *They* may, can, or must be.

PAST TENSE.

	Singular.	Plural.
INDEFINITE	1. *I* might, could, would, or should be.	1. *We* might, could, would, or should be.
	2. *Thou* mightst, couldst, wouldst, or shouldst be.	2. *You* might, could, would, or should be.
	3. *He* might, could, would, or should be.	3. *They* might, could, would, or should be.

PRESENT PERFECT TENSE.

Singular.	Plural.
1. *I* may, can, or must have been.	1. *We* may, can, or must have been.
2. *Thou* mayst, canst, or must have been.	2. *You* may, can, or must have been.
3. *He* may, can, or must have been.	3. *They* may, can, or must have been.

PAST PERFECT TENSE.

Singular.	Plural.
1. *I* might, could, would, or should have been.	1. *We* might, could, would, or should have been.
2. *Thou* mightst, couldst, wouldst, or shouldst have been.	2. *You* might, could, would, or should have been.
3. *He* might, could, would, or should have been.	3. *They* might, could, would, or should have been.

IMPERATIVE MOOD.

PRESENT TENSE.

Singular.	Plural.
Be (*thou*).	Be (*ye* or *you*).

INFINITIVE MOOD.

PRESENT TENSE—To Be.

PAST PERFECT TENSE—To have been.

PARTICIPLES.

PRESENT—Being. | PAST—Been.

COMPOUND PAST—Having been.

243.

CONJUGATION OF THE REGULAR TRANSITIVE VERB "TO CALL."

BOTH VOICES AT ONE VIEW.

ACTIVE VOICE.

INDICATIVE MOOD.

PRESENT TENSE.

	Singular.	*Plural.*
INDEFINITE	1. *I* call or do call.	*We* call or do call.
	2. *Thou* callest or dost call.	*You* call or do call.
	3. *He* calls or does call.	*They* call or do call.

PROGRESSIVE—*I* am calling, *thou* art calling, &c.

Interrogative Form—Do *I* call? Dost *thou* call? &c.

Emphatic Form—*I* do call, *thou* dost call, &c. (Emphasis on '*do.*')

PAST TENSE.

	Singular.	*Plural.*
INDEFINITE	1. *I* called or did call.	*We* called or did call.
	2. *Thou* calledst or didst call.	*You* called or did call.
	3. *He* called or did call.	*They* called or did call.

PROGRESSIVE—*I* was calling, *thou* wast calling, &c.

Interrogative Form—Did *I* call? Didst *thou* call? &c.

Emphatic Form—*I* did call, *thou* didst call, &c. (Emphasis on '*did.*')

PASSIVE VOICE.

INDICATIVE MOOD.

PRESENT TENSE.

	Singular.	*Plural.*
INDEFINITE	1. *I* am called.	*We* are called.
	2. *Thou* art called.	*You* are called.
	3. *He* is called.	*They* are called.

PROGRESSIVE—*I* am being called, *thou* art being called, &c.

Interrogative Form—Am *I* called? Art *thou* called? Is *he* called? &c.

Emphatic Form—(Wanting).

PAST TENSE.

	Singular.	*Plural.*
INDEFINITE	1. *I* was called.	*We* were called.
	2. *Thou* wast called.	*You* were called.
	3. *He* was called.	*They* were called.

PROGRESSIVE—*I* was being called, *thou* wast being called, &c.

Interrogative Form—Was *I* called? Wast *thou* called? &c.

Emphatic Form—(Wanting).

FUTURE TENSE (Signs, **Shall** and **Will**.)

Unemphatic—*denoting mere futurity.*

INDEFINITE		
1.	*I* **shall call.**	*We* **shall call.**
2.	*Thou* **wilt call.**	*You* **will call.**
3.	*He* **will call.**	*They* **will call.**

PROGRESSIVE—*I* **shall be calling,** *thou* **wilt be calling,** &c.

Interrogative Form—**Shall** *I* **call?** **Shalt** *thou* **call?** **Will** *he* **call?** &c.

Emphatic—*denoting purpose, obligation,* &c.

INDEFINITE—*I* **will call,** *thou* **shalt call,** *he* **shall call,** &c.

PROGRESSIVE—*I* **will be calling,** *thou* **shalt be calling,** &c.

Interrogative Form—**Shall** *I* **call?** **Wilt** *thou* **call?** **Shall** *he* **call?** &c.

PRESENT PERFECT TENSE (Sign, **Have**).

1.	*I* **have called.**	*We* **have called.**
2.	*Thou* **hast called.**	*You* **have called.**
3.	*He* **has called.**	*They* **have called.**

PROGRESSIVE—*I* **have been calling,** *thou* **hast been calling,** &c.

Interrogative Form—**Have** *I* **called?** **Hast** *thou* **called?** &c.

FUTURE TENSE (Signs, **Shall** and **Will**.)

Unemphatic—*denoting mere futurity.*

INDEFINITE		
1.	*I* **shall be called.**	*We* **shall be called.**
2.	*Thou* **wilt be called.**	*You* **will be called.**
3.	*He* **will be called.**	*They* **will be called.**

PROGRESSIVE—(Wanting).

Interrogative Form—**Shall** *I* **be called?** **Shalt** *thou* **be called?** **Will** *he* **be called?** &c.

Emphatic—*denoting purpose, obligation,* &c.

INDEFINITE—*I* **will be called,** *thou* **shalt be called,** &c.

PROGRESSIVE—(Wanting).

Interrogative Form—**Shall** *I* **be called?** **Wilt** *thou* **be called?** **Shall** *he* **be called?** &c.

PRESENT PERFECT TENSE (Sign, **Have**).

1.	*I* **have been called.**	*We* **have been called.**
2.	*Thou* **hast been called.**	*You* **have been called.**
3.	*He* **has been called.**	*They* **have been called.**

PROGRESSIVE—(Wanting).

Interrogative Form—**Have** *I* **been called?** **Hast** *thou* **been called?** &c.

PAST PERFECT TENSE (Sign, Had).

	Singular.	Plural.
1.	*I* had called.	*We* had called.
2.	*Thou* hadst called.	*You* had called.
3.	*He* had called.	*They* had called.

PROGRESSIVE—*I* had been calling, *thou* hadst been calling, &c.

Interrogative Form—Had *I* called? Hadst *thou* called? &c.

FUTURE PERFECT TENSE (Signs, Shall have and Will have).

Unemphatic—*denoting mere futurity.*

1.	*I* shall have called.	*We* shall have called.
2.	*Thou* wilt have called.	*You* will have called.
3.	*He* will have called.	*They* will have called.

PROGRESSIVE—*I* shall have been calling, *thou* wilt have been calling, &c.

Interrogative Form—Shall *I* have called? Shalt *thou* have called? Will *he* have called? &c.

Emphatic—*denoting purpose, obligation, &c.*

EMPHATIC FORM—*I* will have called, *thou* shalt have called, *he* shall have called, &c.

Interrogative Form—Shall *I*, wilt *thou*, and shall *he* have called? &c.

PAST PERFECT TENSE (Sign, Had).

	Singular.	Plural.
1.	*I* had been called.	*We* had been called.
2.	*Thou* hadst been called.	*You* had been called.
3.	*He* had been called.	*They* had been called.

PROGRESSIVE—(Wanting).

Interrogative Form—Had *I* been called? Hadst *thou* been called? &c.

FUTURE PERFECT TENSE (Signs, Shall have and Will have).

Unemphatic—*denoting mere futurity.*

1.	*I* shall have been called.	*We* shall have been called.
2.	*Thou* wilt have been called.	*You* will have been called.
3.	*He* will have been called.	*They* will have been called.

PROGRESSIVE—(Wanting).

Interrogative Form—Shall *I* have been called? Shalt *thou* have been called? Will *he* have been called? &c.

Emphatic—*denoting purpose, obligation, &c.*

EMPHATIC FORM—*I* will have been called, *thou* shalt have been called, *he* shall have been called, &c.

Interrogative Form—Shall *I*, wilt *thou*, and shall *he* have been called? &c.

SUBJUNCTIVE MOOD.

PRESENT TENSE.

	Singular.	Plural.
INDEFINITE.	1. (If, though, &c.) *I* call.	(If, though, &c.) *we* call.
	2. (If, though, &c.) *thou* call.	(If, though, &c.) *you* call.
	3. (If, though, &c.) *he* call.	(If, though, &c.) *they* call.

PROGRESSIVE—(If, though, &c.) *I* be calling, (If, though, &c.) *thou* be calling, &c.

PAST TENSE.

	Singular.	Plural.
INDEFINITE.	1. (If, though, &c.) I called.	(If, though, &c.) *we* called.
	2. (If, though, &c.) *thou* calledst.	(If, though, &c.) *you* called.
	3. (If, though, &c.) *he* called.	(If, though, &c.) *they* called.

PROGRESSIVE—(If, though, &c.) *I* were calling, &c.

PRESENT PERFECT TENSE (Sign, Have).

Singular.	Plural.
1. (If, though, &c.) *I* have called.	(If, though, &c.) *we* have called.
2. (If, though, &c.) *thou* have called.	(If, though, &c.) *you* have called.
3. (If, though, &c.) *he* have called.	(If, though, &c.) *they* have called.

PROGRESSIVE—(If, &c.) *I* have been calling, &c.

SUBJUNCTIVE MOOD.

PRESENT TENSE.

	Singular.	Plural.
INDEFINITE.	1. (If, though, &c.) *I* be called.	(If, though, &c.) *we* be called.
	2. (If, though, &c.) *thou* be called.	(If, though, &c.) *you* be called.
	3. (If, though, &c.) *he* be called.	(If, though, &c.) *they* be called.

PROGRESSIVE—(Wanting).

PAST TENSE.

	Singular.	Plural.
INDEFINITE.	1. (If, though, &c.) *I* were called.	(If, though, &c.) *we* were called.
	2. (If, though, &c.) *thou* wert called.	(If, though, &c.) *you* were called.
	3. (If, though, &c.) *he* were called.	(If, though, &c.) *they* were called.

PROGRESSIVE—(If, &c.) *I* were being called, &c.

PRESENT PERFECT TENSE (Sign, Have).

Singular.	Plural.
1. (If, though, &c.) *I* have been called.	(If, though, &c.) *we* have been called.
2. (If, though, &c.) *thou* have been called.	(If, though, &c.) *you* have been called.
3. (If, though, &c.) *he* have been called.	(If, though, &c.) *they* have been called.

PROGRESSIVE—(Wanting).

NOTE.—The form of the remaining Tenses is the same in the Subjunctive as in the Indicative Mood.

POTENTIAL MOOD.

PRESENT TENSE (Signs, **May, Can, Must**).

	Singular.	Plural.
INDEFINITE	1. *I* can call.	*We* can call.
	2. *Thou* canst call.	*You* can call.
	3. *He* can call.	*They* can call.

PROGRESSIVE—*I* can be calling, *thou* canst be calling, &c.

Interrogative Form—Can *I* call? Canst *thou* call? &c.

Use in a similar manner '**May**' and '**Must.**'

PAST TENSE (Signs, **Might, Could, Would, Should**).

	Singular.	Plural.
INDEFINITE	1. *I* could call.	*We* could call.
	2. *Thou* couldst call.	*You* could call.
	3. *He* could call.	*They* could call.

PROGRESSIVE—*I* could be calling, *thou* couldst be calling, &c.

Use in a similar manner '**Might,**' '**Would,**' and '**Should.**'

PRESENT PERFECT TENSE (Signs, '**May have,**' '**Can have,**' '**Must have**').

Singular.	Plural.
1. *I* can have called.	*We* can have called.
2. *Thou* canst have called.	*You* can have called.
3. *He* can have called.	*They* can have called.

PROGRESSIVE—*I* can have been calling, *thou* canst have been calling, &c.

Use in a similar manner '**May have**' and '**Must have.**'

POTENTIAL MOOD.

PRESENT TENSE (Signs, **May, Can, Must**).

Singular.	Plural.
1. *I* can be called.	*We* can be called.
2. *Thou* canst be called.	*You* can be called.
3. *He* can be called.	*They* can be called.

PROGRESSIVE—(Wanting).

Interrogative Form—Can *I* be called? Canst *thou* be called, &c.

Use in a similar manner '**May**' and '**Must.**'

PAST TENSE (Signs, **Might, Could, Would, Should**).

Singular.	Plural.
1. *I* could be called.	*We* could be called.
2. *Thou* couldst be called.	*You* could be called.
3. *He* could be called.	*They* could be called.

PROGRESSIVE—(Wanting).

Use in a similar manner '**Might,**' '**Would,**' and '**Should.**'

PRESENT PERFECT TENSE (Signs, '**May have,**' '**Can have,**' '**Must have**').

Singular.	Plural.
1. *I* can have been called.	*We* can have been called.
2. *Thou* canst have been called.	*You* can have been called.
3. *He* can have been called.	*They* can have been called.

PROGRESSIVE.—(Wanting).

Use in a similar manner '**May have**' and '**Must have.**'

Past Perfect Tense (Signs, '**Might have,' 'Could have,' 'Would have,' 'Should have**').

Singular.	Plural.
1. *I* could have called.	*We* could have called.
2. *Thou* couldst have called.	*You* could have called.
3. *He* could have called.	*They* could have called.

Use in a similar manner '**Might have,' 'Would have,' 'Should have.**'

IMPERATIVE MOOD.

Present Tense.

Call (*thou*).	**Call (*ye or you*).**

INFINITIVE MOOD.

Present Tense.

Indefinite—**To call.**
Progressive—**To be calling.**

Past Tense.

Perfect—**To have called.**
Progressive—**To have been calling.**

PARTICIPLES.

Simple Present—**Calling.**

Compound Past—**Having called.**

Past Perfect Tense (Signs, '**Might have,' 'Could have,' 'Would have,' 'Should have.**'

Singular.	Plural.
1. *I* could have been called.	*We* could have been called.
2. *Thou* couldst have been called.	*You* could have been called.
3. *He* could have been called.	*They* could have been called.

Use in a similar manner '**Might have,' 'Would have,' 'Should have.**'

IMPERATIVE MOOD.

Present Tense.

Be (*thou*) called.	**Be (*ye* or *you*) called.**

INFINITIVE MOOD.

Present Tense.

Indefinite—**To be called.**
Progressive—(Wanting).

Past Tense.

Perfect—**To have been called.**
Progressive—(Wanting).

PARTICIPLES.

Compound Present—**Being called.**
Simple Past—**Called.**
Compound Past—**Having been called.**

244. ## CONTRACTED CONJUGATION OF THE IRREGULAR TRANSITIVE VERB "TO SMITE."

Tense.	ACTIVE VOICE.	PASSIVE VOICE.
	INDICATIVE MOOD.	
PRES.	INDEF.—*I* smite, *thou* smitest, &c.	*I* am smitten, *thou* art smitten, &c.
	PROG.—*I* am smiting, *thou* art smiting, &c.	*I* am being smitten, *thou* art being smitten, &c.
	PERF.—*I* have smitten, *thou* hast smitten, &c.	*I* have been smitten, *thou* hast been smitten, &c.
PAST.	INDEF.—*I* smote, *thou* smotest, &c.	*I* was smitten, *thou* wast smitten, &c.
	PROG.—*I* was smiting, *thou* wast smiting, &c.	*I* was being smitten, *thou* wast being smitten, &c.
	PERF.—*I* had smitten, *thou* hadst smitten, &c.	*I* had been smitten, *thou* hadst been smitten, &c.
FUTURE.	INDEF.—*I* shall smite, *thou* wilt smite, &c.	*I* shall be smitten, *thou* wilt be smitten, &c.
	PROG.—*I* shall be smiting, *thou* wilt be smiting, &c.	
	PERF.—*I* shall have smitten, *thou* wilt have smitten, &c.	*I* shall have been smitten, *thou* wilt have been smitten, &c.
	SUBJUNCTIVE MOOD.	
PRES.	INDEF.—(If) *I* smite, (if) *thou* smite, &c.	(If) *I* be smitten, (if) *thou* be smitten, &c.
	PROG.—(If) *I* be smiting, (if) *thou* be smiting, &c.	
	PERF.—(If) *I* have smitten, (if) *thou* have smitten, &c.	(If) *I* have been smitten, (if) *thou* have been smitten, &c.
PAST.	INDEF.—(If) *I* smote, (if) *thou* smote, &c.	(If) *I* were smitten, (if) *thou* wert smitten, &c.
	PROG.—(If) *I* were smiting, (if) *thou* wert smiting, &c.	(If) *I* were being smitten, (if) *thou* wert being smitten, &c.

POTENTIAL MOOD.

Tense.		Active	Passive
PRES.	INDEF.	*I* may or can smite, *thou* mayst or canst smite, &c.	*I* may or can be smitten, *thou* mayst or canst be smitten, &c.
	PERF.	*I* may or can have smitten, *thou* mayst or canst have smitten, &c.	*I* may or can have been smitten, *thou* mayst or canst have been smitten, &c.
PAST.	INDEF.	*I* might smite, *thou* mightest, &c.	*I* might be smitten, *thou* mightest, &c.
	PERF.	*I* might have smitten, *thou* mightest, &c.	*I* might have been smitten, *thou* mightest, &c.

IMPERATIVE MOOD.

Active	Passive
Smite (*thou*).	Be (*thou*) smitten.

INFINITIVE MOOD.

		Active	Passive
PRES.	INDEF.	To smite.	To be smitten.
	PROG.	To be smiting.	
PAST.	PERF.	To have smitten.	To have been smitten.
	PROG.	To have been smiting.	

PARTICIPLES.

Active	Passive
SIMPLE PRESENT—Smiting.	COMPOUND PRESENT—Being smitten.
	SIMPLE PAST—Smitten.
COMPOUND PAST—Having smitten.	COMPOUND PAST—Having been smitten.

SYNTAX.

INTRODUCTORY MATTER.

245. SYNTAX teaches—

(*a*) How words are formed into **Sentences**;

(*b*) How the **words** in a Sentence are **related** to each other; and

(*c*) How **Sentences** are **related** to each other.

246. In dealing with 'Classification' and 'Inflection,' incidental reference was made to the chief combinations of the parts of speech with each other. These are as follow:—

1. A **Finite Verb** with the Noun or Pronoun used as **Subject**;

2. A **Transitive Verb** with the Noun or Pronoun used as **Object**;

3. An **Adjective** with the **Noun** which it distinguishes or describes;

4. An **Adverb** with the **Verb**, **Adjective**, or other **Adverb**, whose meaning it modifies; and

5. **Nouns** (or Pronouns) joined by **Prepositions** to **Verbs**, **Adjectives**, or other **Nouns**.

247. One of the above combinations—viz., that of a **Subject** with a **Finite Verb**, is **essential** to every sentence. This is easy to understand; for a sentence, which is simply '*a fact expressed in words*,' must contain—

1. The name of what we are speaking of; and

2. What we **say** or **state** about the thing spoken of. The former is called the **Subject**; and, being a name, it *must be either* a **Noun** or a **Noun** equivalent. The *latter is* called the **Predicate**; and, being the stating

part of the sentence, it **must either be a Verb**, or **contain a Verb**, this being the only part of speech which **states**. Thus the expression of a fact consists essentially in putting a **naming word** along with a **stating word**; *i.e.*, in combining a *Subject* with a *Finite Verb; e.g.*, "*Wind blows.*"

Notice that the Noun '*wind*' cannot, of itself, express a thought; it is a mere *name*. Observe also that the Verb '*blows*' cannot, of itself, express a thought; for it simply denotes an *action*. But when the **two words** are **put together**, a *meaning* flashes at once upon the mind —a *fact* is expressed—a SENTENCE is formed, viz., "*Wind blows.*"

For further information, see 'Analysis of Sentences.'

248. The leading facts of Syntax are usually expressed in the form of a set of *Rules* and *illustrations*, showing **how to combine and arrange** the parts of speech and their inflections, so as to form correct sentences. These are classed as—

1. **Rules of Concord** or **Agreement**;
2. **Rules of Government**; and
3. **Rules of Arrangement.**

249. If one word be of a certain Case, Gender, Number, or Person, because another word is of that particular Case, Gender, Number, or Person, the two are said **to agree** or to be in **Concord.**

Thus in the sentence "*Thou sleepest,*" the Verb '*sleepest*' is *Second* Person, *Singular* Number, **because** its Subject '*thou*' is *Second* Person, *Singular* Number; '*thou*' and '*sleepest*' are therefore said to agree or to be in concord. Similarly '*his*' and '*lion*' are in concord in "The *lion* seeks *his* prey by night," the word 'his' being *Masculine* Gender and *Singular* Number, **because** 'lion' is *Masculine* Gender and *Singular* Number.

Words in concord may be said to **suit each other.** Notice how unsuited to each other are the following disagreeing words:—'*I writes,*' '*this pens,*' 'the *lion* seeks *her* prey by night.'

250. By **Government** we mean that one word **obliges** another to be of some particular Case or Mood.

Thus a **Transitive Verb** causes its Direct Object to

be in the **Objective Case**; *e.g.*, "John hurt *me*" (not "John hurt *I*").

251. Arrangement is the placing of words in a sentence. Words are properly placed when they convey the **exact sense intended**. Observe how the position of the word '**only**' affects the meaning of the following sentence:—

You *only* are permitted to attempt six questions.
You are *only* permitted to attempt six questions.
You are permitted *only* to attempt six questions.
You are permitted to attempt *only* six questions.

RULES OF SYNTAX.

SUBJECT AND VERB—CONCORD.

252. General Rule.—A Verb **must agree** with its Subject in **Number** and **Person**; as, "*I am;*" "*Thou art;*" "*He is;*" "*Thou walkest;*" "The *boys walk*."

'*They am*' is incorrect, because '*they*' is Third Person, Plural Number, and '*am*' is First Person, Singular Number. Similarly, 'The *boys walks*' is incorrect, for '*walks*' is Singular, and '*boys*' is Plural.

1. The **Subject** is often called the **Nominative to the Verb**, because it is usually a Noun or a Pronoun in the Nominative Case.

2. When we speak of a Verb as having Number and Person, we mean only that it **alters its form** to suit itself to certain changes in the Number and Person of its Subject. Thus, if in the sentence, '*I sleep*,' the Pronoun '*I*' (First Person) be changed to '*thou*' (Second Person), a corresponding change must be made on the form of the Verb in order to make the words suit each other; *e.g.*, '*Thou sleepest*.' Again, if in the sentence '*He sleeps*,' the Pronoun '*he*' (Singular Number) be changed to '*they*' (Plural), the Verb '*sleeps*' becomes '*sleep*'; thus, '*They sleep*.' This is therefore all that is meant by saying—

1. That a **Verb has Number and Person**; and
2. *That it* **agrees with its Subject in Number and *Person*.**

SPECIAL RULES.

253. The following are Special Rules, which should be carefully learned and remembered :—

1. When two or more Singular Subjects are connected by '**and**,' the **Verb should be Plural** ; as,

"*John* AND *James read* well."
"*Jane* AND *Mary are* diligent girls."
"*Ignorance* AND *idleness lead* to vice."

To this rule there are the following exceptions :—

(*a*) When the Singular Subjects connected by '**and**' denote **one idea** or the **same individual**, the Verb should be **Singular** ; as,

"The *mind* AND *spirit remains* invincible."
"*Bread* AND *butter is* wholesome."

"A *laggard* in love, AND a *dastard* in war,
Was to wed the fair Ellen of brave Lochinvar."

(*b*) When a Verb **is followed by several** Singular Nominatives connected by '**and**,' it usually agrees in the **Singular** with the first only ; as,

"Now *abideth faith*, hope, and charity."

2. When two or more Singular Subjects are joined by '**or**,' '**nor**,' or '**as well as**,' the Verb is **Singular** ; as,

"*John* OR *James is* in the house."
"Neither *Frank* NOR *Arthur writes* well."
"The *earth*, AS WELL AS the *moon*, *is* round."

3. When two Subjects or Nominatives of **different Numbers** or **Persons** are joined by '**or**' or '**nor**,' the Verb agrees with the **nearer Nominative** ; as,

"Neither *he* NOR *I am* fit for the task."
"*Are* the *pupils* OR the *master* to blame?"
"NEITHER the *captain* NOR the *sailors were* saved."

NOTE.—In such cases the *Plural* Nominative should be placed *next* the Verb.

4. *When* the **Subject is a Collective Noun**, the Verb

G

is put into either the **Singular** or the **Plural Number**, according as **unity** or **plurality of idea is prominent**; as,

"The *parliament meets* next week."
"The *jury were* divided."

In other words, when the objects denoted by a Collective Noun are regarded as a **whole**, the Verb should be **Singular**; but when attention is called to the **separate members** of the collection, the Verb should be **Plural**.

5. When the **Infinitive Mood**, a **phrase**, or a **sentence** is made the **Subject**, the Verb should be **Singular**; as, "*To win is* pleasant." "*His winning the prize was* creditable to him." "*That he won the prize was* creditable to him."

Phrases and sentences thus used are equivalent to Nouns, and are called respectively **Noun-Phrases** and **Noun-Sentences**. They may stand either as the Subject or the Object of a Verb.

254. Observations. — The words **riches**, **alms**, and **means**, are frequently used with a Singular Verb; but it should be observed that the **s** in **alms** and the **es** in **riches** are not Plural signs, the original words being *ælmesse* (Saxon) and *richesse* (French), both Singular. The **s** in **means** and **news**, is a sign of the Plural. **Means** may take a Verb in either the Singular or the Plural; as, "The *means was* good" (denoting *one* instrumentality); or, "The *means were* good" (denoting more than one). **News** is always put with a Singular Verb; as, "Are ye sure the *news is* true?"

ARRANGEMENT OF THE SUBJECT.

255. GENERAL RULE. The Subject **usually precedes** the Verb; as,

"*Grass* GROWS in the fields."
"*Cows* EAT grass."

256. To this rule there are many exceptions. For *example, the* Subject follows the Verb—

1. *In* **Questions** and **Commands**; as,

"ARE the *apples* ripe?"
"TAKE *you* my place."
"COME hither" = "COME (*thou*) hither."

2. When the introductory Adverb **'there'*** precedes the Verb; as,

"There WAS a *man* named Nicodemus."
"There AROSE a violent *tempest*."

3. Often, especially in poetry, when an **emphatic Adverb** stands at the **beginning** of a sentence; as,

"Up JUMPED the *cat*, and down LEAPT the *mouse*."
"Then SANK the *star* of Solyma."
"There STANDS Philip's *farm*."
"Here IS the *river*."

4. When an **emphatic Adjective begins** a sentence; as,

"Great IS *Diana* of the Ephesians."
"Glorious ARE thy *works*."

5. When the **Subjunctive** with **'If'** understood **begins** a sentence; as,

"WERE *I* Brutus."

6. In such expressions as **'said he,' 'thought I,' &c.**; *e.g.*,

"Trim, SAID my *uncle Toby*."

Exercise 23.

Correct the following errors:—

Good pupils loves their books. James and John learns their lessons. That eminent teacher and scholar were buried yesterday. The bow and arrow were once used as an instrument of war. Either idleness or stupidity are the cause of his bad fortune. Neither the soldiers nor the general are to blame. Neither the general nor the soldiers is to blame. You say you art a better soldier. The council has subscribed for a portrait of their chairman. The head and front of my offending have this extent, no more. The children and I am in the garden. A great writer and eminent critic have said. The dog and the cat does not agree. The news he brought were good. The song of birds are sweet.

---

* In the following sentence notice the difference of meaning between '*there*' used idiomatically to introduce a sentence, and the same word used as an Adverb of Place: "John was baptizing in Ænon, because *there* was much water there."

AGREEMENT BY APPOSITION.

257. General Rule.—When two or more Nouns or a Noun and a Pronoun, denoting the **same person** or **thing**, come together in the **same Sentence**, they agree in Case by **apposition**; as,

"Be kind to *Tray*, the *house-dog*."
"*Luke*, the beloved *physician*, greets you."
"*I*, *John*, was in the isle which is called Patmos."

Sometimes a Noun is put in apposition with a **sentence**; *e.g.*, "JOHN IS ATTENTIVE, a *fact* which accounts for his rapid progress." Sometimes a sentence is put in apposition with a **Noun**; *e.g.*, "What accounts for John's rapid progress is the FACT *that he is diligent*."

258. The Verb '**To Be**' takes the **same case after it as before it**; *e.g.*,

"*I* AM *he*" (*I* and *he* both Nominative).
"*He* IS a good *man*" (*he* and *man* both Nominative).
"I proved *him* TO BE a good *man*" (*him* and *man* both Objective).

259. Several Verbs act like '**To Be**' in this respect. For example—

1. The Verbs—to **seem**, **become**, **appear**, and some others, take a **Nominative before** and a **Nominative after** them, as, "The *cat* SEEMS a *pet*" (*cat* and *pet* both Nominative). Similarly, "*John* APPEARS a lively *boy*." "*James* BECAME a *clerk*." "*Tom* STRUTS a *soldier*."

2. The Verbs—to **call**, **name**, **make**, **create**, **appoint**, and some others, when used in the **Passive Voice**, take a **Nominative before** and a **Nominative after** them; *e.g.*, "The *child* IS CALLED *John*" (*child* and *John* both Nominative). Similarly, *Sir Thomas* IS APPOINTED *Chairman*. "*Mr. Hayes* WAS MADE *President*." "*James* IS CONSIDERED an honest *man*." "*Mr. Disraeli* WAS CREATED an *Earl*."

260. The agreeing words before and after all such Verbs, denote the **same person** or **thing**. This, which *may be considered* a kind of apposition, explains why *they agree*. Observe, however, that when a Verb is used

reflectively, the Noun and Pronoun before and after it, denote the same person or thing, but do not agree in Case; *e.g.*, "*John* has hurt *himself*." "The *spring* will
Nom. Obj. Nom.
uncoil *itself*."
Obj.

Exercise 24.

(*a*) Correct the following errors, and, in each instance, quote the rule which you apply.

That is him. I suspected it to be he. Is it me you wish to speak to? Napoleon, him who died at St. Helena, was a native of Corsica. Whom do men say that he is? It was them who told me. Whom do you think it was? Perhaps it was her. Joan of Arc, her who was burned by the English at Rouen, was an enthusiast. He proved it to be they that were in fault.

(*b*) Point out the **agreeing Cases** in the following, and show why they agree.

I have been your friend for many years. John, who seems a delicate boy, is a very earnest student. Smith became a rich man after he was made a partner in the firm. Who do they say I am? Did you ever hear how John's penny grew a shilling? Ignorance is the cause of much vice. If John were not a coward, he would not be a truant. James remained a clerk to the end of his days. I find John to be the most diligent worker in the class. Mr. B. has been elected member for the county. He will prove a good representative. Among the stones I stood a stone.

PRONOUN AND ANTECEDENT.

261. GENERAL RULE.—**Pronouns** agree in **Number, Gender**, and **Person**, with the **Nouns** for which they stand; as,

"JANE is diligent, *she* learns *her* lessons."
"JOHN came late, *he* was detained by the way."
"JAMES and FRANK were in the GARDEN; *they* say that *it* is full of TREES *which* are covered with fruit."

262. The above rule includes the two following special rules:—

1. A **Relative Pronoun** must agree with its **antecedent** in Gender, Number, and Person; as, "*I who* am your teacher;" "THOU *who* art my pupil;" "BOYS *that steal* are bad companions."

2. When the antecedent consists of two or more Nouns or Pronouns in the **Singular Number** connected by '**and**,' the Relative must be **Plural**; as,

"*He* AND *I who* were present, saw the occurrence."
"I met *John* AND *James who* were going to school."

263. The Relative need not be of the same Case as its antecedent. The **Case** of the Relative depends upon its **relation** either to the **Verb** or to some **Noun** or **Preposition** in its own clause. The two following rules should be understood and committed to memory :—

1. The Relative is the **Nominative to the Verb** in its own clause, **if no other Nominative comes between** the Relative and the Verb; as,

"He *that* IS virtuous, is happy."
"The girl *who* WON the prize, received it."

2. If a Nominative comes between the Relative and the Verb, then the **Relative** is either in the **Objective Case** governed by **the Verb following** or by **a Preposition going before**, or in the **Possessive Case** governed **by a Noun following**; as,

"He *whom* we WORSHIP, by *whose* GIFT we live, and BY *whom* all things were made, is the Lord."

264. The Relative '**that**' should be preferred to '**who**' or '**which**' in the following cases :—

1. **After superlatives**; as, "The FINEST music *that* ever you heard." The BEST poem *that* ever was written."
2. If the **antecedent consists of two words**, one denoting a **person** and the other **not**; as,

"The MAN and the ASS *that* I met."

265. SUPPRESSION OF THE RELATIVE, &c.

1. The Relative, when in the **Objective Case**, is **frequently omitted**; as, "The boy I met by the way" = "The boy *whom* I met by the way." "The pen I am writing with" = "The pen *which* I am writing with."
2. In poetry we find the Relative **occasionally omitted in the Nominative Case**; as,

"*What* is this absorbs me quite?" =
"*What* is this *which* absorbs me quite?"

"There are twenty of Roslin's barons bold,
Lie buried within that proud chapelle."
"Lie buried" = "*Who* lie buried."

3. The **antecedent** is **often omitted** in **poetry**; *e.g.*,

"*Who* lags for dread of daily work,
Commits a folly and a crime."
"*Who* lags" = "*He who* lags."

4. The Relative '**what**' includes both the antecedent and the Relative; thus, "Did you hear *what* was said?" = "Did you hear *that which* was said?"

Parse '*that*,' Objective Case governed by '*did hear*,' and *which*, Nominative Case to the Verb '*was said*.'

Another way of parsing this sentence is to take '*what*' as Nominative to '*was said*,' and '*what was said*,' as the Object of '*did hear*.'

Exercise 25.

(*a*) **Correct** the following errors:—

O Thou who are the leader of Israel. He is the best boy whom I have in my class. I am the man who teach you. I who speaks to you am the person. That is the girl who I gave the pen to. The boy and the dog which were lost have been found. He was the first who died. The bravest soldier who was in the camp could not have been more fearless. I am the man who love his friends. I am the man, who loves my friends. It is he who speakest to you.

(*b*) Tell the **Gender, Number,** and **Person** of the Pronouns in the following:—

John is a boy who has a good mind. Did you do the exercises which I appointed? John, who they thought was their enemy, proved himself a friend. Jane is a girl whose truthfulness is admired. His language was the same as I have used. Have you got what you wanted? Jane and Mary are two girls that work diligently. His arguments were as follow.

(*c*) Supply and parse the **omitted Relatives.**

The barge she sat in burned on the water. The youth came to order the thin toast the landlord spoke of. The man I asked could give me no information. Where is the boy I gave my book to? Did you post the letter I gave you? James is a boy everybody likes. Remember the lesson I taught you.

"You are the man must bring our babes
To wealth or misery."

ADJECTIVE AND NOUN.

266. GENERAL RULE.—**Every Adjective refers to a Noun** or **something equivalent to a Noun**; as,

"Horses are *noble* ANIMALS, THEY are *useful* also."
"TO DRIVE is *pleasant* on a warm day."

1. When the quality expressed by an Adjective is **affirmed** or **denied** (predicated) of the Noun, the Adjective is said to be used **predicatively**; as,

"Sugar is *sweet*." "Milton was *blind*."

2. The Adjective is used predicatively after to **be**, **seem**, **become**, **appear**, and certain other **Intransitive Verbs**; *e.g.*, "The bird seems *tame*." "John has grown *rich*." "Frank is not *proud*, although he has become *eminent*." "Thomas proved *deceitful*."

3. When an Adjective is put **close to the Noun**, it is said to be used **attributively**; as, "The *feathery* palm-trees." "The *sunny* skies." "The twilight *cold* and *gray*."

4. In the **attributive relation**, the quality expressed by the Adjective, is **simply ascribed** or **attributed** to the Noun, not predicated of it. But **all Adjectives** (Participles included), whether expressing quality or not, are considered **attributive** when put **close to** the Noun; *e.g.*, "*A* slate." "*The* pen." "*That* man." "*Two* men." "*No* men." "*His* books." "Men *wounded* in battle."

267. The attributive relation is also expressed by means of—

1. A **Noun** in the **Possessive Case**; as, "*John's* hat."

2. **A Noun** in **apposition**; as, "James, *the blacksmith*."

3. A **Noun** preceded by the Preposition **of**; as, "A man *of wisdom*."

4. A **descriptive phrase** joined to a Noun by means of a **Preposition**; as, "The man *with the umbrella* is my cousin."

5. A **descriptive sentence** introduced by a **Relative** *Pronoun*; as, "The storm *that was foretold*, did not happen."

These all play the part of Adjectives, because their function is to describe Nouns. Call a phrase describing a Noun, an **ADJECTIVE-PHRASE**; and a sentence describing a Noun, an **ADJECTIVE-SENTENCE.**

268. CONCORD OF ADJECTIVE AND NOUN.

1. **This** and **that** agree in Number with the Nouns which they point out; as,

"*That man;*" "*Those houses.*"

These are the **only Adjectives** in English, which agree with the Noun by **inflection**. They are also used as Pronouns.

2. **Each, every, either,** and **neither** are Singular, and must be followed by a Verb, a Noun, or a Pronoun, in the Singular; as,

"*Each* person *walks* past in *his* turn."
"But *every* man in *his* own order."
"*Either* of the two *is* able to do it."
"*Every man, woman,* and *child was* saved."

Each, either, and **neither** are often used as Pronouns. **Either** is a Pronoun in the above example. **Every**, in ordinary language, is seldom a Pronoun.

ARRANGEMENT OF ADJECTIVES.

269. RULE I. When the Adjective is used **attributively**, its natural place is **immediately before the Noun** which it qualifies; as, "A *green* field;" "A *good* scholar."

Exceptions.—The natural order is departed from in such cases as the following:—

(*a*) When the Adjective **is combined with some word or phrase** which modifies its meaning; as, "A MAN *worthy* of respect." "A PUPIL *anxious* to please." "A WALL six feet *high*. "A BOY ten years *old*."

(*b*) When **several Adjectives** are connected with the **same Noun**; as, "A COUNTRY *great, glorious,* and *free.*" "A MAN wise, learned, and respected."

(*c*) When the Adjective is **qualified by an Adverb**, it often follows its Noun; as, "A SERVANT strictly *honest*." "A PERSON scrupulously *exact*."

(*d*) When the Adjective is used as a **title**; as, "ALFRED the *Great*;" "WILLIAM the *Silent*."

RULE 2. When the Adjective is used **predicatively**, its natural place is **after** such Verbs as—to **be**, to **seem**, to **appear**, to **become**, to **remain**, &c.; as,

"James IS *clever*." "He WILL BECOME *famous*."

Exception.—But when it is desired to give **emphasis** to the Adjective, this order is inverted; as,

"*Green* BE thy fields." "*Rich* and *rare* WERE the gems she wore." "*Great* IS Diana of the Ephesians."

Exercise 26.

(*a*) **Distinguish** the Adjectives used **attributively** from those used **predicatively**.

(*b*) Pick out the **Adjective-Phrases** and the **Adjective-Sentences**.

No useless coffin enclosed his breast. Few and short were the prayers which we said. There in the twilight cold and gray, lifeless but beautiful he lay. Hear the words of wisdom, which the wise man utters. Look at little Willie with his many pretty wiles. The way was long, the wind was cold. The person who told me is truthful. You yet may spy the fawn at play. I flew to the pleasant fields traversed so oft in life's morning march when my bosom was young. The judge on the bench must be respected. Who is the tall man at the wheel, that steers the ship? Our English archers bent their bows, their hearts were good and true. The tale which you relate seems incredible. James, who was once a lazy boy, has become diligent and attentive. Our efforts have proved successful. I have a large dog that barks fiercely. The fable of the dog in the manger describes the behaviour of many a selfish, quarrelsome person. A bird in the hand is sure. The story of the man in the moon is a mere myth. I met a whining schoolboy with his satchel. He is a man of intellect, but he has a heart of stone.

VERB AND OBJECT.

270. GENERAL RULE.—**Transitive Verbs in the *Active Voice* govern the Objective Case of Nouns and *Pronouns*; as,**

"Good pupils *respect* their *masters*."
"The master *praised me*."

271. In the Active Voice, the Verbs, to **call, name, appoint, make, create, esteem, elect**, &c., govern **two Objectives** of the **same** person or thing; as,

"They APPOINTED *him teacher*." "They CALLED the *child James*." "They MADE *him president*." "I CONSIDER *Henry* a good *boy*."

Notice here that both Objects are Direct, and that the second is **descriptive** or **complementary** of the first. When Verbs of this class are changed to the Passive Voice, the **two Objectives** become **two Nominatives**, one before the Verb and the other after it; thus, "They MADE *him president*" (*him* and *president* both Objective). "*He* WAS MADE *president*" (*he* and *president* both Nominative).

272. The Verbs—**give, tell, buy, sell, teach, send, ask, lend**, and some others, are followed in the Active Voice by **two Objectives**, one of **a person** and the other of a **thing**; as,

"I GAVE *him* a *present*." "He SENT *me* a *flower*." "FORGIVE *us* our *debts*." "He ASKED *her* a *question*." "I TAUGHT *them grammar*."

1. The **Objective of the thing** is the **Direct** Object; the **Personal Object is Indirect**, for you may govern it by a Preposition understood; *e.g.*,

"Give *me* a *pen*" = "Give (to) *me* a *pen*."
"Teach *me* my *duty*" = "Teach (to) *me* my *duty*."
"I asked *him* a *question*" = "I asked (of) *him* a *question*."
"Saddle *me* the *ass*" = "Saddle (for) *me* the *ass*."

2. The two Objects which follow Verbs of *teaching* and *asking* are regarded by some grammarians as being both Direct. Verbs of *teaching* and *asking* are followed in Latin by two Direct Objects. In English, however, it is better to consider every Object as Indirect, which can be explained by supplying a Preposition to govern it, as in the above examples.

3. When Verbs of this kind are used in the Passive Voice, the **Personal Object most frequently becomes the Nominative** to the Verb, the other remaining as a Direct Object following after; as,

"The master TAUGHT *him grammar*" = "*he* WAS TAUGHT *grammar* by the master."

4. But **either Object** may be made the **Subject**, the other being retained as an Objective after the Passive Voice, with its **relation to the Verb unchanged**; *e.g.*, "*He* WAS SAVED the *trouble*;" or, "The *trouble* WAS SAVED *him*." "*He* WAS REFUSED the *favour*; or, "The *favour* WAS REFUSED *him*." "*He* WAS FORGIVEN the *debt*;" or "The *debt* WAS FORGIVEN *him*."

INTRANSITIVE VERBS—THE OBJECT.

273. The following rules regarding Intransitive Verbs are both interesting and important:—

1. **Intransitive Verbs** become **Transitive**, if followed by a **Noun akin in meaning**; as,

"He DIES the traitor's *death*."
"He LAUGHED a *laugh* of merry scorn."
"They SLEPT their *sleep* outright."
"The disease RAN its *course*."

2. Intransitive Verbs become **Transitive**, if used in a **causative** sense; as,

"He TROTTED the *pony*" (*trotted* = *caused* to trot).
"Let us FLY our *kites*" (*fly*=*cause* to fly).

3. Some Intransitive Verbs become Transitive by the addition of a **Preposition**; *e.g.*, "Fortune *smiled on* him." "The people *laughed at* him."

"*To smile on*" and "*to laugh at*" are each to be considered as one Verb; (1) because it takes the Verb and the Preposition to express the one idea which is before the mind; and (2) you may use "*to laugh at*" and "*to smile on*" in the Passive Voice; thus, "He *was smiled on* by fortune;" "He *was laughed at* by the people."

These are called **Prepositional or Compound Transitive** *Verbs*.

4. An Objective Case denoting **Adverbial** relation, and answering such questions as, **When ?**, **How long ?**, **How far ?**, **How much ?**, **How old ?**, is put along with some Verbs (chiefly Intransitive), and some Adjectives. This is called the **Adverbial** Objective. A Preposition may usually be inserted before it.

EXAMPLES: "He DIED last *week*." "He WAITED an *hour*." "He CAME the shortest *way*." He WALKED a *mile*," "His youthful hose well saved, a *world* TOO WIDE." "He is ten *years* OLD." "*Summers* two I am OLDER, Anne, than you." "He came forth BOUND *hand* and *foot*."

IMPERSONAL VERBS, &c.

274. An **Impersonal Verb** is one used with 'IT' as **Subject**. Some Impersonal Verbs are followed by a Direct, and others by an Indirect Object; *e.g.*,

"*It grieves me* greatly" (*me*, Direct Object).

"*It becomes you* to be earnest" (*you* = *for you*, Indirect Object).

1. '**Me**' in '**methinks**' and '**meseems**' is an Indirect Object. "*Methinks* I hear a spirit in your echoes" = "*It seems to me* I hear," &c. '**Thinks**' in '**methinks**' is not a part of the ordinary Verb 'To THINK,' but an impersonal use of an old Verb, 'THINCAN' = "*To seem* or *appear*."

2. '**Chase**' and '**day**' are Indirect Objects in—

"Woe WORTH the *chase*, woe WORTH the *day*,
That cost his life, my gallant gray."

'**Worth**' is here Third Person Imperative of an old Verb, 'WEORTHAN' = to befall or happen.

"Woe WORTH *the chase*" = "Woe HAPPEN *to the chase*."

THE INFINITIVE AS AN OBJECT.

275. The **Infinitive Mood** is governed by **Verbs**, **Nouns**, or **Adjectives**; as, John LIKES *to study*." "I READ *to learn*." "Your DESIRE *to succeed* is praiseworthy." "Are you ANXIOUS *to remain?*"

1. Sometimes the **Infinitive** is a **Direct Object**; *e.g.*, "John LIKES *to study*" = "John LIKES studying or *study*."

2. When the Infinitive **expresses a purpose**, or is governed by a **Noun or an Adjective**, it is to be parsed as an **Indirect Object**, because it is equivalent, in such cases, to an Abstract Noun governed by the Preposition '*for*.' Thus, "I read *to learn*" = "I read *for learning*." "He is ready *to go*" = "He is ready *for going*." "His desire *to improve*" = "His desire *for improvement*."

This is often called the Dative Infinitive, being equivalent to the Dative Case in Latin.

276. ARRANGEMENT OF THE OBJECT.

1. When the Object is a **Noun** or a **Personal** Pronoun, it naturally **follows** the Verb which governs it; as,

"Brutus KILLED *Cæsar*."
"James HELPED *me*."

2. When the Object is a **Relative** Pronoun it **precedes** the Finite Verb which governs it; as,

"I have the pen WHICH you *lost*."
"James is a boy THAT I *like*."

3. The Object is **emphasised** by taking it out of its natural order and placing it at the beginning of a sentence; as,

"*Him* I HAVE CHOSEN."
"*Money* I WANT, and *money* I CRAVE" (Christmas Rhyme).

Exercise 27.

Parse the following sentences syntactically, and quote the rules of Syntax which you apply:—

You have often obliged me. I saw you and him. John lent me his pen. Mr. Moore sent John a present. They named the child Alfred. The girl was appointed a pupil-teacher. The master forgave him his fault. I was asked a question which I could not answer. Teach me to feel another's woe. Mr. Brown teaches his boys music. You should love your neighbour as yourself. It behoves John to be very watchful. It pains me to see so many idle boys. The question was asked me before. John showed me the house where he lives. I was shown the house where John lives. John is an honest man. My friends will leave next Friday. The bridge of wood stood a furlong from the door. Thomas has lived ten years in that house. They went their way. *May we* live the life and die the death of the righteous. We *bought the farm* we tenanted before. Edmund thought money a *dead thing*. There stands Philip's farm where brook and river meet. Who are you? Who shall I say called? Get what you can, and what you get hold. The river flowed over the meadow. The land was overflowed by the river. James is willing to go. John does not like to be from home.

PREPOSITION AND OBJECT.

277. GENERAL RULE.—**Prepositions** are followed by the **Objective Case** of Nouns and Pronouns; as,

"The ship sails ON the *sea*."
"Give that TO *me*."

1. When the Object is a **Relative** or an **Interrogative** Pronoun, it often precedes the Preposition; as,

"The pen *which* I am writing WITH."
"*What* are you thinking OF?"

2. Prepositions often govern a **group of words** equivalent to a Noun; as,

"He is accused OF *betraying his friend*."

3. The Preposition is **understood**—

(*a*) Before the **Indirect Object**; as,

"Lend *me* a pen" = "Lend *to me* a pen."

(*b*) After certain **Interjections**; as,

"Ah *me!*" = "Ah *for me!*"
"Woe is *me!*" = "Woe is *to me!*"

THE POSSESSIVE CASE.

278. GENERAL RULE.—A Noun or Pronoun in the **Possessive Case** is governed by a **Noun**, or the **equivalent of a Noun**, following after it; as,

"That is *James's* HOUSE."
"This is *my* PEN."
"*John's* ATTENDING SO WELL is in his favour."

1. Sometimes the governing Noun is **understood**; *e.g.*,

"Call at the *grocer's*" (*grocer's* = *grocer's* SHOP).
"I passed *St. Paul's*" (*St. Paul's* = St. Paul's CHURCH).

2. The following use of the Possessive is **idiomatical**:

"He is a friend *of my father's.*"
"That is a book *of my sister's.*"

Such expressions are proper only when they can be explained thus:—

"He is a friend *of my father's*" = "He is a friend *out of my father's friends*" = "He is *one of my father's friends.*" "That is a book *of my sister's*" = "That is a book *out of my sister's books*" = "That is *one of my sister's books.*"

The **Possessive** stands as an **attribute** to the Noun which governs it. See § 267.

ADVERB AND VERB, ADJECTIVE, OR ADVERB.

279. Adverbs are joined to Verbs, Adjectives, or other Adverbs, to express relations of **time, place, manner,** &c.; as,

"He WILL *soon* return."
"Come *hither*, my little page."
"He *often* ACTS *very rashly.*"
"The sun is *very* BRIGHT."

280. Adverbial relations are also expressed by means of—

1. **Phrases introduced by Prepositions**; *e.g.*,

"He came *at twelve o'clock*" (time).
"He spoke *with great energy*" (manner).
"William is digging *in the garden*" (place).

2. **Clauses or sentences**; *e.g.*,

"The ship sailed *when the tide was full*" (time).
"You will find the book *where you left it*" (place).
"He acts *as a good boy should act*" (manner).
"*The wind being favourable*, we set sail" (cause).

3. Phrases and sentences which denote adverbial relations, are called **Adverb-Phrases** and **Adverb-Sentences** respectively.

281. Observations.—1. An Adverb may modify an Adverb-Phrase; as,

"He arrived JUST *at that moment.*"
"The ball hit the target EXACTLY *in the centre.*"

2. Sometimes an Adverb modifies a sentence; as,

"PERHAPS *I shall go to-morrow.*"
"FORTUNATELY, *we did not travel by that train.*"

3. Adverbs such as **only, even, not,** are often used partly as Adjectives; as,

"*Only a fool* would act so."
"*Even chronometers* fail to keep exact time."
"*Not a word* was spoken" (*not a* = *no*).

ARRANGEMENT OF THE ADVERB.

282. The Adverb may be **shifted about** more than any other part of speech without disturbing the sense of the sentence; but to prevent ambiguity, it is usual to place it as close as possible to the word which it modifies.

As a general rule, Adverbs are placed—

1. **After** simple Verbs; as,

"He ACTED *justly.*" "He SLEPT *soundly.*"

2. **After** compound Verbs in the Active Voice; as,

"He SHOULD HAVE WRITTEN *more carefully.*"

3. **Before** the **Principal Verb** in the Passive Voice; as,

"The copy SHOULD HAVE BEEN *carefully* WRITTEN."
"It IS *very badly* EXECUTED."

4. **Before** Adjectives and other Adverbs; as,

"John is *too* ANXIOUS."
"He has laboured *very* DILIGENTLY."

Caution.—The Adverbs '**even**' and '**only**' are often **misplaced**, which gives rise to ambiguity. Thus: "The address *only* to be written on this side," is ambiguous; it should be "*Only* the address, &c." Similarly, "Homer *even* sometimes nods," should be "*Even* Homer sometimes nods."

283. MISCELLANEOUS RULES.

1. When a Noun or Pronoun stands as the name of **anything addressed**, it is said to be in the **Nominative of Address**; as,

"O *king*, live for ever!"
"Come here, *Samuel*."
"O *earth*, what changes thou hast seen!"

2. When a Noun or Pronoun **precedes a Participle** without being connected, as **Object or Subject** with any Finite Verb, it is said to be in the **Nominative Absolute**; as,

"The *wind* BEING favourable, we set sail."
"We shall not fear, *thou* LEADING."

3. The **Infinitive Mood** and the **Present Participle** are often used **absolutely**; as,

"*To be* candid with you, I think you are in error."
"Humanly *speaking*, there is no hope of his recovery."

4. The following construction with '**than**' and the **Objective Case of the Relative**, should not be imitated:

"Alfred, THAN *whom* a greater king never reigned."

5. The Conjunction '**than**' follows the **Comparative Degree** of Adjectives and Adverbs; as,

"SWEETER *than* honey." "STRONGER *than* a lion."
"I would RATHER go *than* remain."

6. Some Conjunctions occur in **pairs**; as,

"*Though* deep, *yet* clear."
"I cannot say *whether* he will come *or* not."
"*Either* John *or* James will bring it."
"He will judge *both* the quick *and* the dead."

7. **Two Negatives** in the same simple sentence, are equivalent to an **affirmative**; as,

"I will *not* take *no* more" = "I will take *some* more."

8. As a general rule, **the Tense of Auxiliary Verbs in dependent sentences** should agree with the Tense of the Verb in the **principal sentence**; as,

"I *tell* you I *will* do it if I can."
"I *told* you I *would* do it if I could."

"He *says* he *may* be here to-morrow."
"He *said* he *might* be here to-morrow."
"John *says* he *can* work Fractions."
"John *said* he *could* work Fractions."

Exercise 28.

Parse syntactically the following Sentences, and **quote the rules of Syntax** which you apply :—

The bird's nest was robbed by a bad boy. I have been at the hatter's buying a hat for John. Pull the primrose, sister Anne! That is a favourite saying of my mother's. The clamour of the church's being in danger was revived. This done, Mazeppa spread his cloak. God save thee, ancient Mariner!

"The parents being dead and gone,
The children home he takes."

"Earth! render back from out thy breast
A remnant of our Spartan dead."

"O joyous birds! it hath still been so,
Through the halls of kings doth the tempest go."

To speak the truth, we are all imperfect. Strictly speaking, Relative Pronouns have no Gender. Sir King, I closed mine eyelids, lest the gems should blind my purpose. One man, in his time, plays many parts, his acts being seven ages.

"The thunder-clouds close o'er it, which when rent,
The earth is covered thick with other clay,
Which her own clay shall cover."

284. FORM OF SYNTACTICAL PARSING.

NOUN.—1. *Kind* (Proper, Common, or Abstract); 2. *Number*; 3. *Gender*; 4. *Case*, and how *related* to another word in the sentence—whether as a *Subject*, an *Object* (Direct or Indirect), or an *Attribute*.

PRONOUN.—1. *Kind* (Personal, Relative, &c.); 2. *Person*; 3. *Number*; 4. *Gender*; 5. *Case*, and how *related* to another word in the sentence.

ADJECTIVE.—1. *Kind*; 2. *Degree of Comparison*; 3. The *Noun* or *Noun equivalent* to which it belongs; 4. How *used*—whether as an *Attribute* or a *Predicate*.

VERB.—1. *Kind* (Transitive or Intransitive); 2. *Conjugation* (Regular or Irregular); 3. Voice (Active or Passive); 4. *Mood*; 5. Tense; 6. Person; 7. Num-

ber; 8. *Agreeing with*; 9. *Government*, if Transitive and in the Active Voice. A *Compound Verb* must of course be treated as *one Verb;* but in order to show its structure, the *Auxiliary* or *Auxiliaries* and the *Principal Verb* which compose it, should also be parsed separately.

ADVERB.—1. *Kind*; 2. *Degree of Comparison*; 3. The *Verb*, *Adjective*, or other *Adverb* which it modifies.

PREPOSITION.—The *words* which it *connects*.

CONJUNCTION.—1. *Kind;* 2. The *sentences* which it *connects*.

285. EXAMPLE OF PARSING—(1).

Hard by a spreading lime-tree stood,
To this the youth was bound;
They placed an apple on his head;
He looked in wonder round.
"The fault is mine, if fault there be,"
Cried Tell in accents wild;
On manhood let your vengeance fall,
But spare, oh, spare my child!"

Hard by.........A Compound Adverb of Place, modifying the Verb '*stood*.'

a....................An Adjective of Number, referring indefinitely to the Noun '*lime-tree*'—called also the Indefinite Article.

spreading........An Adjective of Quality, Positive degree, referring attributively to the Noun '*lime-tree*.'

lime-tree.........A Common Noun, Sing. number, Neuter gender, and Nom. case, being the Subject of the Verb '*stood*.'

stood..............An Intransitive Verb, Irreg., Act. voice, Indic. mood, Past-Indefinite tense, Third pers., Sing. number, agreeing with its Subject '*lime-tree*.'

to....................A Preposition, joining the Pronoun '*this*' to the Verb '*was bound*.'

this................A Demonstrative Pronoun, Sing. number, and Object. case, being the Object of the Prep. '*to*.'

the.................A Demonstrative Adjective, pointing out the Noun '*youth*'—called also the Definite Article.

youth.............A Common Noun, Sing. number, Mascul.* gender, and Nominative case, being the Subject of the Verb '*was bound*.'

---

* *Known to be* Masculine from the sense of the passage, but not from *the form of the* word which is, strictly speaking, applicable to either sex.

was bound ...A Transitive Verb, Irregular, Passive voice, Indic. mood, Past-Indef. tense, Third pers., Sing. number, agreeing with its Subject '*youth.*' This Verb is made up of the Auxiliary '*was*' and the Principal Verb '*bound,*' which are parsed thus:

was............The Indic. mood, Past tense of the Auxiliary Verb 'To Be,' Third pers., Sing. number, agreeing with '*youth;*' and used with '*bound*' to form the Passive voice.

bound ....The simple Past Participle, Passive, of the Irreg. Trans. Verb 'To Bind,' used with the Auxiliary '*was*' to form '*was bound,*' a compound stating Verb of the Passive voice.

they ....A Pers. Pronoun, Third pers., Plur. number, Com. gender, and Nom. case, being the Subject of the Verb '*placed.*'

placed ....A Transitive Verb, Regul., Active voice, Indic. mood, Past-Indef. tense, Third pers., Plur. number, agreeing with its Subject '*they.*'

apple ....A Com. Noun, Sing. number, Neut. gender, and Objective case, being the Direct Object of the Trans. Verb '*placed.*'

his..............A Possessive Adjective, referring attributively to the Noun '*head,*' being the Possessive form of the Personal Pronoun 'He.' This word may be parsed as a Pronoun thus: *his*—A Personal Pronoun, Third pers., Sing. number, Masc. gender, and Possess. case, governed by the Noun '*head.*'

head ....A Com. Noun, Sing. number, Neut. gender, and Obj. case, being the Object of the Prep. '*on.*'

he...............A Pers. Pronoun, Third pers., Sing. number, Masc. gender, and Nom. case, being the Subject of the Verb '*looked.*'

looked ....An Intransitive Verb, Reg., Act. voice, Indic. mood, Past-Indef. tense, Third pers., Sing. number, agreeing with its Subject '*he.*'

round ....An Adverb of Place, modifying the Verb '*looked.*'

fault ....An Abstract Noun, Sing. number and Nom. case, being the Subject of the Verb '*is.*'

is ....A Neuter and Irreg. Verb, Indic. mood, Present Indef. tense, Third pers., Sing. number, agreeing with its Subject '*fault.*'

mine ....A Possessive Pronoun, standing for '*my fault,*' First pers., Sing.* number, and Nom. case,

---

* Because '*fault,*' which the word implies, is Sing. number, and not because '*mine*' denotes *one person.* Thus, '*mine,*' '*yours,*' &c., are Singular or Plural according to whether it is *one* thing or *more than one* thing which is possessed. For example, "*mine is* as good as yours;" "*mine are* as good as yours;" "*yours is* as good as mine;" "yours are as good as mine."

coming after the Verb '*is*.' This word may also be parsed thus:—*Mine*—A Personal Pronoun, First pers., Sing.* number, Possessive case, governed by the Noun '*fault*;' or thus:—*Mine*—A Possessive Adjective, referring predicatively to the Noun '*fault*.'

NOTE.—Any of these three ways of parsing '*mine*,' and all similar words may be regarded as correct. The last, perhaps, should be preferred.

if..................A Conditional Conjunction, connecting the sentences, "The fault is mine," and "there be fault."

there..............The Introductory or Idiomatic Adverb, joined to the Verb '*be*.'

be..................An Intrans. Verb, Irreg. (no voice since it does not imply an action), Subjunctive mood, Pres. Indef. tense, Third pers., Sing. number, agreeing with its Subject '*fault*.'

cried..............A Trans. Verb,† Reg., Act. voice, Indic. mood, Past Indef. tense, Third pers., Sing. number, agreeing with its Subject '*Tell*.'

Tell................A Proper Noun, &c., Nom. case, being the Subject of the Verb '*cried*.'

in...................A Prep., connecting '*cried*' and '*accents*.'

wild................An Adjective of Quality, Pos. degree, referring attributively to '*accents*.'

let..................A Trans. Verb, Irreg., Act. voice, Imper. mood, Second pers., Sing. number, agreeing with its Subject '*you*' understood.

your...............A Possessive Adj., referring attributively to the Noun '*vengeance*.'

vengeance........An Abstract Noun, &c., Direct Obj. of '*let*.'

fall.................An Intrans. Verb., Irreg., Act. voice, Infinitive mood, Pres. tense, governed by '*let*,' the sign '*to*' being suppressed.

but.................A Contrasting Conjunction, connecting 'On manhood let,' &c., with 'spare, oh, spare,' &c.

spare..............A Trans. Verb., Reg., Act. voice, Imper. mood, Second pers., Sing. number, agreeing with '*you*' understood.

my..................See '*his*' and '*your*.'

child...............A Com. Noun, &c., Obj. case, being Dir. Obj. of '*spare*.'

---

* Because the word '*mine*' denotes a *single person*.

† The Direct Object—viz., *what Tell cried*—should be specially pointed out in an instance like this. It is as follows:—"The fault is mine, if fault *there be; on manhood let your vengeance fall; but spare, oh, spare my child*."

286. EXAMPLE OF PARSING—(2)

This elegant rose, had I shaken it less,
Might have bloomed with its owner a while;
And the tear that is wiped with a little address,
May be followed, perhaps, by a smile.

This ....A Demonst. Adj., pointing out the Noun '*rose.*'

elegant ....An Adj. of Quality, Pos. degree, referring attributively to the Noun '*rose.*'

rose ....A Com. Noun, Sing. number, Neut. gender, and Nom. case, being the Subject of the Verb '*might have bloomed.*'

had shaken...A Trans. Verb, Irreg., Act. voice, Subjunctive mood (*if* understood; thus, *had I* shaken = *if I had* shaken), Past Perf. tense, First pers., Sing. number, agreeing with its Subject '*I.*' This Verb is made up of the Auxiliary '*had*' and the Principal Verb '*shaken,*' which are parsed separately thus:—

had ....The Subjunctive mood, Past tense of the Auxiliary Verb 'To Have,' First pers., Sing. number, agreeing with '*I,*' and used with the Principal Verb '*shaken*' to express the Past Perf. tense of the Verb 'To Shake.'

shaken.........The form called the simple Past Participle of the Irreg. Trans. Verb 'To Shake,' not used here as a Participle, but as the principal part of a stating Verb of the Act. voice; viz., '*had shaken.*'

it ....A Pers. Pron., Third pers., Sing. number, Neut. gender, and Obj. case, being the Dir. Obj. of '*had shaken.*'

less.............An Adv. of Degree, Compar. degree, modifying '*had shaken.*'

might have bloomed } An Intrans. Verb, Reg., Act. voice, Potential mood, Past Perf. tense, Third pers., Sing. number, agreeing with its Subject '*rose.*' This Verb is made up of the Auxiliaries '*might*' and '*have*' and the Principal Verb '*bloomed,*' which are parsed separately thus:—

might.........The Indic. mood, Past tense of the Auxiliary and Defective Verb 'May,' Third pers., Sing. number, agreeing with '*rose;*' and forming with '*have bloomed*' = '(*to*) *have bloomed,*' the Past Perf. Potential of the Verb 'To Bloom.'

have...........The simple Infinitive of the Auxiliary Verb 'Have' governed by '*might,*' and forming with '*bloomed*' the Perf. Infinitive, Act. '(*to*) *have bloomed.*'

bloomed.......The form called the simple Past Participle of the Reg. Intrans. Verb 'To Bloom;' not used here as a Participle, but as the principal part of the stating Verb '*might have bloomed.*'

with............A Prep. connecting the Noun '*owner*' with the Verb '*might have bloomed.*'

its.............A Possess. Adj., referring attributively to '*owner.*'

while...........An Abstract Noun, &c., Obj. case, governed by '*for*' understood, being the Indir. Obj. of '*might have bloomed,*' and denoting 'time how long'?

and............A Cop. Conjunction, connecting the sentence, "This elegant rose, had I shaken, &c.," with "the tear that is wiped with a little address, &c."

tear............A Com. Noun, &c., Nom. case, being the Subject of '*may be followed.*'

that............A Rel. Pron., Antecedent '*tear,*' Third pers., Sing. number, Neut. gender, agreeing with '*tear,*' and Nom. case, being the Subject of '*is wiped.*'

is wiped.......A Trans. Verb, Reg., Pass. voice, Indic. mood, Pres. tense, Third pers., Sing. number, agreeing with its Subject '*that.*' This Verb is made up of the Auxiliary '*is,*' and the Principal Verb '*wiped,*' which are separately parsed thus:—

is..............The Indic. mood, Pres. tense of the Auxiliary Verb 'To Be,' Third pers., Sing. number, agreeing with '*that,*' and used with '*wiped*' to form the Passive voice.

wiped.........The simple Past Participle Passive, of the Reg. Trans. Verb 'To Wipe,' used as the Principal Verb with the Auxiliary '*is,*' to form '*is wiped,*' a compound stating Verb of the Passive voice.

with............A Preposition connecting the Noun '*address*' with the Verb '*is wiped.*'

little...........An Adj. of Quantity, Pos. degree, referring attributively to the Noun '*address.*'

may be followed A Trans. Verb, Reg., Passive voice, Potential mood, Pres. tense, Third pers., Sing. number, agreeing with its Subject '*tear.*' This Verb is made up of the Auxiliaries '*may*' and '*be,*' and the Principal Verb '*followed,*' which are parsed separately thus:—

may...........The Indic. mood, Pres. tense of the Auxiliary and Defective Verb 'May,' Third pers., Sing. number, agreeing with its Subject '*tear;*' and forming with '*be followed*' = '*(to) be followed*' the Pres. Potential Passive of the Reg. Trans. Verb 'To Follow.'

be = to be....The simple Infinitive of the Auxiliary Verb 'Be,' and forming with '*followed*' the Pres. Infinitive Passive '*(to) be followed.*'

followed......The simple Past Participle Passive of the Reg. Trans. Verb 'To Follow,' used as the Principal

Verb with the Auxiliaries '*may*' and '*be*' to form '*may be followed*,' a compound stating Verb of the Passive voice.

perhaps..........An Adverb of Degree, modifying the statement, '*The tear may be followed by a smile*,' showing *to what extent* it is to be regarded as a *fact*.

by................A Prep., connecting the Noun '*smile*' with the Verb '*may be followed*.'

smile.............A Common Noun, &c., Objective case, governed by the Prep '*by*.'

Exercise 29.

Parse the following Sentences according to the above models:—

With fire and sword the country round was wasted far and wide. Hast thou forgot the day when my father found thee first in places far away (call '*far away*' a compound Adj. qual. *places*)? But half of our heavy task was done when the bell tolled the hour for retiring (call '*but*' an Adv., and '*retiring*' a Verbal Noun or Gerund). "Try not the pass!" the old man said; "dark lowers the tempest overhead." The sweet face of Lucy Gray will never more be seen. Many flocks were on the hills, but thou wert owned by none (parse '*wert owned*' the Indicative mood with a Subjunctive form). Hail to thee, blithe spirit! bird thou never wert. The mayor was dumb, and the council stood as if they were changed into blocks of wood. Poor creature, can it be that 'tis thy mother's heart which is working so in thee? Perish policy and cunning; perish all that fears the light.

ANALYSIS OF SENTENCES.*

287. A **Sentence** has already been defined as a group of words conveying a complete sense or meaning. Statements, questions, commands, entreaties, &c., are sentences. See § 6.

A **single word** sometimes conveys a complete meaning, and is then the equivalent of a sentence; *e.g.*, '**Yes**' and '**No**,' used as answers. See § 103.

Many **Interjections** are **condensed sentences**; *e.g.*,

"Adieu!"="I commend you to God."
"Good-bye!"="God be with you."
"Up!"="Get up."
"Forward!"="Go forward.

Words of this sort are called **Word-sentences**.

---

* The word *analysis* is the English form of the Greek word ἀνάλυσις (analusis) = an unloosing.

Sentence is derived from Lat. *sententia* = a judgment, a meaning.

288. To **analyse** a sentence means—

1. To **separate it** into its parts; and
2. To show **the relation of the parts** to each other.

289. It has been already shown (§ 247) that a sentence may be broken up into two parts:—

1. The *name* of what we are speaking of.
2. *What we say about* the thing spoken of.

The name of what we are speaking of is called the **Subject**.

What we say about the Subject is called the **Predicate**.

In the sentence "Rain falls," '*rain*' is the name of what we are speaking of, and we say of the rain that it '*falls;*' therefore '*rain*' is the Subject, and '*falls*' the Predicate. Similarly—

Subject.	Predicate.
Trees	grow.
Sugar	is sweet.
Rivers	run into the sea.
Birds	sing in the woods.

THE SUBJECT.

290. The grammatical or **Simple** Subject is always either a **Noun** or **Pronoun** in the Nominative Case, or some **word group** equivalent to a Noun; *e.g.*,

Simple Subject.	Predicate.
John	is diligent.
He	is faithful.
Walking	is healthful.
To walk	is healthful.
To be punctual	is commendable.
That he acted wisely	is admitted.

291. The **Enlarged** Subject.—The Simple Subject may be **enlarged** in the following ways:—

1. By an **Adjective**; as,

Good water	is wholesome.
The green fields	are beautiful.

2. By a **Descriptive Phrase** equivalent to an Adjective (see § 267); as,

The man *at the helm*	is skilful.
Men *of wisdom*	are respected.
The lessons *for to-morrow*	are easy.

3. By a **Noun** or **Pronoun** in the Possessive Case; as,

John's hat	is new.
Your dog	barks fiercely.
My head	aches.

4. By an **Adjective Sentence** (see § 267); as,

Henry, *who answered best,*	got the prize.
The house *where I live*	is being painted.
The reason *why he did so*	is not clear.

5. By a **Noun in Apposition**; as,

Burns, *the poet,*	was a Scotchman.
James, *the postman,*	brought the letter.
Paul, *the apostle,*	was very zealous.

You will notice that the **Enlargements**—called also attributes—merely define or describe the Subject, and are therefore either Adjectives or Adjective equivalents.

292. **Model for Analysis**—(1.)

Enlarged Subject.	Predicate.
John's new and costly watch Solomon, the son of David, James, who saw the occurrence,	fell on the floor. built the temple. remembers it.

Model for Analysis—(2.)

The Subject.		Predicate.
Simple Subject.	Enlargements.	
Watch, Solomon, James,	John's, new, costly, the son of David, who saw the occurrence,	fell on the floor. built the temple. remembers it.

Exercise 30.

Analyse the following Sentences according to Model (2):—

Little drops of water make up the ocean. A friend in need is a friend indeed. Alexander the Great, the son of Philip, conquered Persia. A strong desire to excel is to be commended. John's horse, which he bought lately, is very gentle. Children, coming home from school, look in at the open door.

THE PREDICATE.

293. The **Predicate** is what is **said** or **affirmed** of the Subject. It must therefore contain the chief Verb of the sentence. An Intransitive Verb, or a Transitive Verb in the Passive Voice, may form a **complete** Predicate; as,

"Lions *roar.*" "The river *runs.*"
"The letter *is written.*" "Lincoln *was shot.*"

294. The Verb 'TO BE' cannot, of itself, form a Predicate, except when it means **to exist**, as in the sentence, "God *is*"="God *exists.*" We must therefore join some word or words to it to make the Predicate; *e.g.*,

"The moon *is round.*" "James *is a sailor.*"
"I *am he.*" "She *is here.*" "He *is to go.*"
"The camel *is of a light-brown colour.*"

The Verbs 'to **seem**,' 'to **become**,' &c., resemble the Verb 'TO BE' in this respect; *e.g.*,

"He *seems prudent.*" "Paul *became a Christian.*"

Notice that when the Verb 'TO BE' is used to express mere existence, it is usually preceded by the introductory Adverb 'THERE;' *e.g.*,

"*There was* light"="Light *was* or *existed.*"
"*There is* hope"="Hope *exists.*"
"*There are* many suns"="Many suns *exist.*"

THE OBJECT OR COMPLETION.

295. The Verb which stands grammatically related to the Subject, is called the **Simple** Predicate. When the latter is a Transitive Verb in the Active Voice, the Object must, of course, be added to make the sense *complete.* The Object is therefore called the **Completion of the Predicate.**

The Object must be a **Noun**, or a **Pronoun**, or a **group of words** equivalent to a Noun. Like the Subject, it may be **enlarged** by Adjectives or Adjective equivalents.

296. Some Verbs (271, 272) require two Objects to complete the sense, and both are, of course, included in the Completion of the Predicate. Remember that sometimes both Objects are Direct; and that sometimes one is Direct, and the other Indirect. The latter is usually governed by 'to' or 'for' expressed or understood, and is thus easily recognised.

The Infinitive Mood is often one of the two Objects; as, "I taught *James to parse.*" But observe that the Infinitive is only a part of a single Direct Object in, "I like *a rascal to be punished;*" "I believe *John to be an honest man.*" The Infinitive, in such expressions, plays the part of a Finite Verb; for, "I like *a scoundrel to be punished*" = "I like *that a scoundrel should be punished.*" See § 194 (*c*).

NOTE.—The pupil learning Latin, should compare this form of the Object with the Latin construction called the 'Accusative before the Infinitive.'

297. MODEL FOR ANALYSIS—(3.)

SUBJECT.	COMPLETE PREDICATE.	
	VERB OR SIMPLE PREDICATE.	OBJECT OR COMPLETION.
James	has worked	his sum.
He	promised	to behave better.
Frank	sent	John (*Indir. Obj.*) a book. (*Dir. Obj.*)
They	appointed	him (*Dir. Obj.*) teacher. (*Dir. Obj.*)

Exercise 31.

Analyse the following Sentences according to Model (3):—

Children should obey their parents. Boys like to be amused. James asked John where he had been. William says, "Keep up *your heart.*" The master promised me a book. I heard the loud *thunder rolling.* The Queen created him a baronet. Saddle me

the ass. They saddled him the ass. The committee appointed Mr. B. secretary. I know your works. I have heard how you acted. Harry's heart could not contain itself. Mr. B. asked the little boy his name. The magistrate ordered the dog to be shot.

ADVERBIAL EXTENSIONS OF THE PREDICATE.

298. Adverbs, and phrases or sentences doing the duty of Adverbs, may be added to the Predicate to mark the **time, place, manner**, or **instrument** of the action which the Verb expresses. These additions are usually called **Extensions of the Predicate**. They are all classed after the manner of Adverbs.

299. Examples of Extensions, denoting—

(*a*) **Time**................ "He came *twice*."
"John staid *for a whole week*."
"The doctor comes *when he is sent for*."

(*b*) **Place**................ "Kaspar sat *outside*."
"Kaspar sat *before his cottage door*."
"Kaspar sat *where the sun shone*."

(*c*) **Manner**............ "John behaves *well*."
"He does his work *in a thorough manner*."
"He acts *as a gentleman should act*."

(*d*) **Cause**.............. "He came *to tell me*."
"He ran *to ask what he had found*."
"John will succeed *because he is diligent*."

(*e*) **Instrument**....... "The horse was killed *by lightning*.
"The country was wasted *with fire and sword*."
"The boy writes *with a pen*."

(*f*) **Accompanying Circumstances** "Kempenfelt went down *with twice four hundred men*."
"Nelson sailed to the Baltic *with a large fleet*."
"Wellington defeated Napoleon at Waterloo, *notwithstanding that the latter was at the head of a larger army*."

NOTE.—Extensions of Instrument and Accompanying Circumstances, are usually included under Manner (*c*).

300. Extensions of **Time** answer—**When? How long? How often?**
Extensions of **Place** answer—**Where? Whither? Whence?**
Extensions of **Manner** answer—**How? How much?**
Extensions of **Cause** answer—**Why?**
Extensions of **Instrument** answer—**With what?**

301. **MODEL FOR ANALYSIS—(4.)**

THE SUBJECT.	THE PREDICATE.		
	VERB OR SIMPLE PREDICATE.	OBJECT OR COMPLETION.	ADVERBIAL EXTENSIONS.
He	**heard**	**the news,**	this morning (*time*).
James, who was sharply reproved yesterday,	wrote	his copy	1. to-day (*time*). 2. with great care (*manner*).
Wellington, the Iron Duke, the hero of a hundred fights,	was buried	...	1. in St. Paul's (*place*). 2. with princely honours (*manner*). 3. on the 18th Nov. 1852 (*time*).

Exercise 32.

Analyse the following Sentences according to Model (4):—

Alexander conquered Darius, king of Persia, in his own dominions, in the year 330 B.C. My father lived at Blenheim then, yon little stream hard by. The gondola glides, like a spirit of night, o'er the slumbering waves in the calm moonlight. The hounds ran swiftly through the woods, the nimble deer to take. About a week ago, a woodman with his axe felled a large tree in that park, the owner and some visitors being present to see the operation. O'er Roslin all that dreary night, a wondrous blaze was seen *to gleam*. They carved at the meal with gloves of *steel*.

SENTENCES.

302. Sentences are of three kinds—

1. **Simple** Sentences.
2. **Compound** Sentences.
3. **Complex** Sentences.

303. A **Simple** sentence contains but **one Subject** and **one Finite Verb**; as,

1. "*Rivers* RUN."
2. "The broad and deep *sea* SEPARATES us."
3. "Many large and useful *trees* GROW in Great Britain."

304. When two words denoting the same thing, and connected by the Conjunction 'OR,' stand as the Subject, the sentence must be considered as Simple; *e.g.*,

1. The *sovereign* OR *ruler* of Britain IS a Queen.
2. The *core* OR *heart* of the apple IS decayed."
3. "A *vane* OR *weathercock* TURNS with every wind."

[Notice that 'OR,' in such cases, connects words and not sentences; and is therefore not disjunctive. Also that 'AND' connects words in the "The *broad* AND *deep* sea divides us;" viz., the two Adjectives '*broad*' and '*deep*,' qualifying one Subject '*sea*.' This is interesting, as 'AND' and 'OR' are the only Conjunctions in the language, that are used to connect words. See § 114.]

COMPOUND SENTENCES.

305. When two or more Simple sentences are so combined that one is **not dependent** on the other for its meaning, they form what is called a Compound sentence; *e.g.*,

"*John sings* AND *James draws.*"
"Frank *is come,* BUT *I have not seen him yet.*"

306. The Simple sentences (called members or clauses) which make up a Compound sentence, are said to be **co-ordinate**, a term denoting that they are of equal *importance*. The Conjunctions which join them together are therefore called **Co-ordinate Conjunctions**. Examples—*and, also, but, neither, nor, either, or*, &c.

307. Compound sentences are often **contracted**; thus, "Jane writes and Mary writes" = "Jane and Mary write." "John did not go and James did not go" = "Neither John nor James did go (went)."

In the analysis of Contracted sentences, you must **supply all omitted words**, so as to show the co-ordinate members of which they consist.

COMPLEX SENTENCES.

308. When one sentence depends upon another for its full meaning, it is called a **Subordinate** sentence, and the one upon which it depends is called the **Principal** sentence. The two taken together form what is called a **Complex** sentence.

Thus, in the Complex sentence, "I know a bank whereon the wild thyme blows," we have two sentences:—

1. "I know a bank."
2. "The wild thyme blows."

But the full meaning of sentence (2) is not perceived until it is joined to sentence (1), by the adverbial Conjunction '*whereon.*'

309. Subordinate sentences are of three kinds—

1. **Noun-sentences.**
2. **Adjective-sentences.**
3. **Adverb-sentences.**

310. A **Noun-sentence** is the **equivalent of a Noun**, and may be used either as the Subject or the Object of a Verb. See p. 98.

Examples — Complex sentences containing **Noun-sentences**:—

1. "*That you have been attentive* IS evident."
2. "I SEE *that you have been attentive.*"
3. "TELL me *where the French live.*"
4. "Do you KNOW *what I am thinking of?*"

311. When a **Noun-sentence** is used as a **Subject**, it is usual to begin the statement with the Pronoun 'IT';' *the Noun-sentence* **preceded by the** Conjunction 'THAT.'

being placed after the Verb. Thus, instead of saying "*Men are mortal* IS a fact," we say "*It* IS a fact *that men are mortal.*" In analysing such expressions, remember that 'it' merely *introduces* and *stands for* the real Subject, which is the Noun-sentence.

312. An **Adjective-sentence** is the **equivalent of an Adjective**, and describes some Noun in the Principal sentence. See § 267.

EXAMPLES—Complex sentences containing **Adjective sentences** :—

1. "The MAN *who is good*, is noble."
2. "I remember the HOUSE *where* (*in which*) *I was born.*"
3. "He saw the PERSON *to whom you refer.*"
4. "The SHIP *that was launched a month ago*, is now ready for sea."

NOTE.—An Adjective-sentence is usually joined to the Principal sentence by means of a **Relative Pronoun** or a **Relative Adverb** (Adverbial Conjunction).

313. An **Adverb-sentence** is the **equivalent of an Adverb**, and is used as such to modify the Verb, or some Adjective or Adverb in the Principal clause. See § 280.

EXAMPLES—Complex sentences containing **Adverb-sentences** :—

1. "You MAY COME *when you please.*"
2. "You MAY GO *where you please.*"
3. "He ACTED *as a gentleman should act.*"
4. "Dublin is a LARGER city *than Belfast* (*is large*)."
5. "John is as TALL *as James* (*is tall*)."
6. "*The more I know of him* the BETTER I like him."
7. "*The wind being favourable* = (*because the wind was favourable*), we SET SAIL."

314. Adverb-sentences are joined to the Principal *clause* by what are called **Subordinate Conjunctions**, *so called* because they introduce Subordinate sentences.

The following are examples:—*Where, when, until, while, since, because, than, as, so as, so that,* &c.

315. In Complex sentences it often happens that a **Subordinate sentence** stands in the position of a **Principal to another clause** depending upon it.

EXAMPLE—"There he learned that his late companion, who had just set off, was the celebrated Mr. Burke."

Here, there are three Simple sentences:—

1. There he learned,
2. that his late companion was the celebrated Mr. Burke,
3. who had just set off.

Sentence (2) is subordinate to sentence (1), for it is a Noun-sentence used as the Object of the Verb '*learned*.' Sentence (3) is subordinate to sentence (2), for it is an Adjective-sentence describing the Subject '*companion*.' Sentence (2) is therefore subordinate to sentence (1), and at the same time a Principal in regard to sentence (3).

METHOD OF ANALYSING **COMPOUND** AND **COMPLEX** SENTENCES.

316. A **GENERAL ANALYSIS** of any Compound or Complex sentence is made by—

(*a*) Dividing it into as many clauses or simple sentences as it contains Subjects or Finite Verbs; and

(*b*) Showing the relation of the clauses to each other.

317. EXAMPLES AND MODEL.

1. When the peace came on I was discharged, and, as I could not work because my wound was troublesome, I enlisted for a landsman in the East India Company's service.

2. The spirit who bideth by himself
In the land of mist and snow,
He loved the bird that loved the man
Who shot him with his bow.

3. "Cast thy eyes eastward," said he, "and tell me *what thou seest*."

General Analysis—Model (5).

No.	Clauses or Simple Sentences.	Kind of Sentenc
1.	*a.* When the peace came on,	Adv. sent. (*time*), sub nate to *b*.
	b. I was discharged,	Prin. sent., co-ord. witl
	c. as I could not work,	Adv. sent. (*cause*), sul to *e*; also a Prin. sent.
	d. because my wound was troublesome,	Adv. sent. (*cause*), sul to *c*.
	e. and I enlisted for a landsman in the East India Company's service.	Principal sentence, co-nate with *b*.
2.	*a.* The spirit (he) * loved the bird,	The Principal sentence.
	b. who (= *the spirit*) bideth by himself in the land of mist and snow,	Adj. sent. subordinate qualifying the Su '*spirit*.'
	c. that (= *the bird*) loved the man,	Adj. sent. subord. to *a*, the Object '*bird*;' a Prin. sent. to *d*.
	d. who (= *the man*) shot him (*the bird*) with his bow.	Adj. sent. subord. to *c*, the Object '*man*.'
3.	*a.* Cast (thou) thy eyes eastward,	Noun sent. subord. t part Object of '*said*.'
	b. he said,	The Prin. sent. whose is *a*, *c*, and *d*, takes gether.
	c. and tell (thou) me,	Noun sent. subord. to *b*, of the Obj. of '*said*;' a Prin. sent. to *d*.
	d. what thou seest.	Noun sent. subord. t Object of '*tell*.'

318. When, in addition to the General Analysis Compound or Complex sentence, the separate cl are analysed, what is called a **Detailed Analy** performed.

A Detailed Analysis may be more or less detail pleasure; and may be conveniently expressed in wr in a tabular form, as in Model 6.

* *Notice* that the Personal Pronoun '*he*' and its antecedent ' *are here* used together as the Subject of the Verb '*loved*.' This st *is permitted* in poetry, when it is desired to emphasise the *It is not* allowable in prose.

319. EXAMPLE—As I was yesterday morning walking with Sir Roger before his house, a country fellow brought him a huge fish, which, he told him, Mr. William Wimble had caught that very morning; and that he presented it with his service to him, and intended to come and dine with him.

TABULAR DETAILED ANALYSIS—MODEL (6.)

SENTENCES.	KIND OF SENTENCE.	SUBJECT AND ENLARGEMENTS.	SIMPLE PREDICATE.	OBJECT AND ENLARGEMENTS.	ADVERBIAL EXTENSIONS.
a. As I was yesterday morning walking with Sir Roger before his house,	Adv. sentence (*time*); subordinate to *b*,	I,	was walking,	...	yesterday morning (*time*), with Sir Roger (*manner*), before his house (*place*).
b. a country fellow brought him a huge fish,	Principal sentence to *a*, and to *c*; also co-ord. with *d*.	a country fellow,	brought	him (*Indirect*), a huge fish (*Direct*),	as I was yesterday morning walking with Sir Roger, &c. (*time*).
c. which Mr William Wimble had caught that very morning,	Adj. sent. subord. to *b*, qual. the Direct Obj. '*fish;*' also sub-ord. to *d*, as part of the Object of '*told*,'	Mr. William Wimble,	had caught,	which (*Direct*),	that very morning (*time*).
d. he told him, &c.	Principal sentence co-ordinate with *b*,	he	told	him (*Indir.*); *c*, *e*, and *f* (*Dir. Obj.*),	
e. and that he presented it with his service to him,	Noun sent. subord. to *d*; being part Object of '*told*,'	he	presented	it (*Direct*),	with his service to him (*manner*).
f. and (that he) intended to come and dine with him.	Noun sentence subordinate to *d*; co-ordinate with *e*,	he	intended	to come and dine with him (*Direct*).	

Exercise 33.

Analyse the following Sentences according to Models 5 and 6:—

The blackening wave is edged with white,
To inch and rock the sea-mews fly;
The fishers have heard the water-sprite,
Whose screams forebode that wreck is nigh.

There is a tide in the affairs of men, which, taken at the flood, leads on to fortune. When people would talk of a rich man in company, Whang would say, "I know him very well." The Accusing Spirit, which flew up to heaven's chancery with the oath, blushed as he gave it in; and the Recording Angel, as he wrote it down, dropped a tear upon the word, and blotted it out for ever. There is not the smallest orb which thou behold'st, but in his motion like an angel sings, still quiring to the young-eyed cherubim. This predecessor of ours, you see, is dressed after this manner, and his cheeks would be no larger than mine were he in a hat as I am. The corporal made his old bow, which usually spoke as plain as a bow could speak it—"Your honour is good."

I dreamed that Greece might still be free;
For, standing on the Persian's grave,
I could not deem myself a slave.

He prayeth best who loveth most,
All things both great and small;
For the dear God who loveth us,
He made and loveth all.

HOW ENGLISH IS RELATED TO OTHER LANGUAGES.

320. Languages have been classified into a few general divisions called FAMILIES. The most important of these is that called the **ARYAN** or **INDO-EUROPEAN FAMILY**, which embraces the languages of India and Persia, and all the European tongues except Finnish, Hungarian, and Turkish. The latter were introduced from Central Asia into Europe, in comparatively recent times, and belong to an entirely different class.

321. The European languages (proper) are separated into the following groups:—

1. The **SLAVONIC**—comprising RUSSIAN, POLISH, and BOHEMIAN.

2. The **Græco-Latin**—comprising (1) Ancient and Modern Greek; (2) Latin and the Latin-derived (Romance) languages, viz.: *Italian, French, Spanish, Portuguese, Wallachian*, and *Romansch.*

3. The **Keltic**—comprising Irish, Gaelic (of the Highlands of Scotland), Manx (of the Isle of Man), Welsh, Cornish (now extinct), and Armorican (of Brittany).

4. The **Teutonic**—comprising (*a*) Modern or High-German (so called because it was first spoken in the *highlands* of Germany).
   (*b*) The Scandinavian languages—*Danish, Icelandic, Swedish*, and *Norwegian.*
   (*c*) The Low-German languages—*Dutch, Frisian, Flemish*, and *English.* The Low-German languages are so called because they were spoken originally by the people inhabiting the *low* plains bordering the German Ocean and the Baltic.

322. **English** therefore belongs to the **Low-German** group of Teutonic languages. In its earliest form it was brought into England by the Angles, Saxons, and Jutes, who migrated thither, in the fifth and sixth centuries, from the shores of the German Ocean. Hence the earliest English is called Anglo-Saxon.

323. The English Dictionary contains a vast number of words derived from Latin, Greek, and other sources, but especially from the Latin. All our most common and useful words, however, are of Teutonic or Saxon origin; and although the language, in many respects, has undergone very great changes since its introduction into the country, yet the Grammar has remained essentially English.

For *examples* of English at different periods, see Dr. Sullivan's English Grammar, page 204 to page 212.

THE ELEMENTS OF OUR VOCABULARY.

324. **The Anglo-Saxon Element.**—The Anglo-Saxon, as might be expected, forms the basis or ground-work of the English Language. All our Pronouns, as *I, thou,*

he, she, who, which, each, every, this, that, are of Saxon origin; also all our Auxiliary Verbs, and most of our Prepositions and Conjunctions; nearly all our most common and useful Adjectives; as *black, white, bad, good, kind*, &c.; and the greater number of our most common and useful Verbs and Nouns; as, *come, go, eat, drink, live, die, sing, work, love, hate, father, mother, brother, sister, man, boy, girl, bird, fowl, sheep, fish.*

325. It is said that about 60 per cent. of the words in an ordinary English Dictionary, are of Saxon origin; but most people, in speaking and writing, use, of Saxon words, a much higher percentage than this.

Most of our monosyllables are from this source; and in such books as the English Bible, the writings of Bunyan, and the works of some of our best poets, the proportion of foreign-derived words is comparatively small. It is said that 75 per cent. of the words in Macaulay's "Essay on Bacon," and nearly 90 per cent. of those used in Tennyson's "In Memoriam," are of Anglo-Saxon origin.

In scientific and philosophical writings the percentage of Saxon words is very much smaller.

326. **The Latin Element.**—Of the vast number of English words traceable to Latin, some have come direct, whilst a larger number have found their way into the language through the medium of French. The Norman Conquest (1066) led to the introduction of a great many Norman-French words. It may be observed, however, that the majority of our Latin-English words have been added since the fifteenth century. This century (towards its close) and the next (the sixteenth), are distinguished for what has been called the REVIVAL OF LEARNING.

A large number of our words of three or more syllables, are of Latin origin; also most of the terms used in theology, medicine, law, and politics.

327. **The Greek Element.**—Many of the terms used in science, philosophy, theology, &c., are from the Greek; as, *hydrogen, thermometer, metaphysics, psychology, analysis, synthesis, aphelion, perihelion, dogma, bishop, christian, catholic, presbyterian, baptism, eucharist.*

328. **The Keltic Element.**—The ancient Britons spoke Keltic; but so completely was their language displaced by that of their Saxon conquerors, that, with the exception of the names of places, few Keltic words became incorporated with the English vocabulary. In Ireland, Scotland, and Wales, most of the names of towns, mountains, capes, rivers, and lakes, are of Keltic origin. In England, the majority of the names of places are Saxon; but the mountains and rivers generally bear Keltic names.

The following common words are from this source—*pan, crag, glen, pail, mop, crock, clout, basket, mattock, bard, whisky, shamrock, flannel, tartan, gruel, glue.*

329. **Miscellaneous Words.**—The English vocabulary has been enriched by miscellaneous words adopted direct from many different languages. Thus—

1. From the **French** we have adopted, without change, such words as—*aide-de-camp, etiquette, naïveté, burlesque, valet, boudoir, escritoire, chemise, charade.*
2. From the **Spanish**—*cigar, embargo, lagoon, negro, mosquito, alligator.*
3. From **Portuguese**—*marmalade, palaver, caste, fetish.*
4. From **Italian**—*pantaloons, charlatan, conversazione.*
5. From the **Dutch**—*sloop, schooner, yacht.*
6. From the **German**—*waltz, mangel-wurzel,* &c.
7. From **Indian** and **Chinese** tongues—*ratan, bamboo, bazar, bungalow, gong, Bohea, Congou.*
8. From **Arabic**—*almanac, algebra, mummy, assassin, syrup, admiral, alchemy, giraffe, gazelle.*
9. From **Persian**—*caravan, scarlet, azure, lilac, paradise, dervish.*
10. From **Turkish**—*scimitar, dragoman, divan.*
11. From **American Indian**—*potato, tobacco, wigwam, tomahawk, squaw, maize, hurricane.*
12. From the **Hebrew**—*cherub, seraph, amen, jubilee, sabbath, Satan;* and Proper names such as, *Elizabeth, Mary, Rachel, John, David, Adam.*

330. TABLE SHOWING HOW ENGLISH IS RELATED TO OTHER EUROPEAN LANGUAGES.

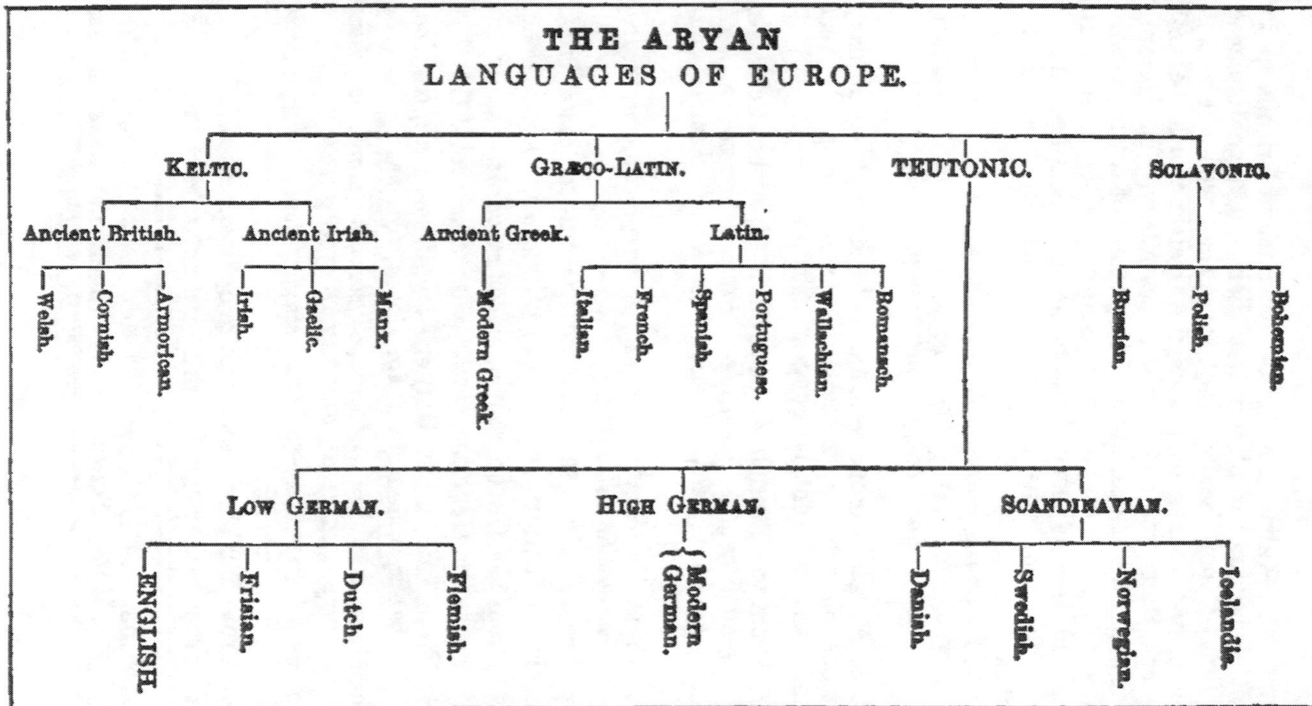

PUNCTUATION.

331. **Punctuation** is the art of dividing written language into **sentences**, or **parts of sentences**, so as to convey the meaning with greater clearness, and to indicate more or less fully the pauses required in reading.

332. The **POINTS**, or Stops, used in English are the following:—

1. The **Comma**, . . [,]	6. The **Note of Interrogation**, . . [?]
2. The **Semicolon**, . [;]	7. The **Note of Exclamation**, . [!]
3. The **Colon**, . . [:]	8. The **Parenthesis**, ( )
4. The **Period**, . . [.]	
5. The **Dash**, . . [—]	

9. The **Quotation Points**, (" ") (' ').

333. The **duration of the pauses** varies according to the nature of the composition; but, generally speaking, the **Comma** denotes a pause about equal to the time required to pronounce a word of **one syllable**; the **Semicolon**, a word of **two syllables**; the **Colon**, a word of **three**; and the **Period**, a word of four.

RULES AND EXAMPLES.

334. In punctuation, the **COMMA** marks the **smallest division** of a sentence.

335. Generally speaking, the **parts of a simple sentence** expressed in natural order, **should not be separated** by any point; as,

"The passion for praise produces excellent effects in women of sense."

"Our interests are interwoven by threads innumerable."

1. But when the **natural order is inverted**, a **Comma** should be placed **between the transposed parts**, unless when the sentence is very short; as,

"*By threads innumerable*, our interests are interwoven."

"Silver and gold have I none."

2. When the **simple sentence** is **long**, the sense is often made clearer by a **Comma before the Verb**; as,

"To be totally indifferent to praise or censure, is a real defect in character."

336. Subordinate sentences, participial clauses, and Adjectives with dependent words, are generally '**pointed off**' from the context by the Comma; as,

"The passion for praise, *which is so very vehement in the fair sex*, produces excellent effects in women of sense."

"To improve time, *whilst we are blessed with health*, will smooth the bed of sickness."

"The king, *approving the plan*, put it into execution."

"But he, *anxious to please*, consented."

1. But Relative and participial clauses taken in a **restrictive** sense, and **immediately following** the words to which they refer, **should not be preceded** by a Comma; as,

"A man *who is of a detracting spirit*, will misconstrue the most innocent words."

"A man *renowned for repartee*
Will seldom scruple to make free
With friendship's finer feelings."

2. Also when the subordinate sentence is **short**, and is **closely connected** with the principal clause, the **Comma** is **unnecessary**; as,

"Revelation tells us *how we may attain happiness*."

337. The **Nominative absolute**, the **Infinitive absolute**, and the **Nominative of address**, are **pointed off** from the context by Commas; as,

"At length, *their ministry performed, and their race well run*, they left the world in peace."

"This is, *to say nothing worse*, highly reprehensible."

"*Friends, Romans, Countrymen*, lend me your ears."

"I am, *Sir*, your obedient servant."

338. When a **Noun** or **Pronoun** with an **Adjective** or **Adjective equivalent** attached to it, is put in ap-

position to another Noun, a Comma should be inserted between them; as,

"It is the lark, *the herald of the morn.*"
"Augustus, *the Roman emperor, he who succeeded Julius Cæsar*, is variously described."

1. But it is **not necessary to insert a Comma**, if the **word in apposition stands alone**; as,

"Milton the *poet* wrote it."
"I *myself* saw it."

339. **Adverb phrases** (especially at the beginning of a sentence), and also **Adverbs modifying**, not single words, but the **whole clause** to which they belong, are usually **separated** from the context by Commas; as,

"*Generally speaking*, I felt satisfied with his conduct."
"His work is, *in many respects*, very imperfect."
"Remember this best friend; *formerly*, the supporter of thy infancy, and the guide of thy childhood."

1. The Adverbs—**again, firstly, secondly, finally, thus, namely, nay,** &c.; and the Conjunctions—**moreover, however,** &c., are usually pointed off from the context by Commas.

340. **Two words** of the same class **connected by a Conjunction**, must not be separated by a Comma; but, when the Conjunction is omitted, a Comma should be put in its stead; as,

"His *father and mother* are in the country." "Jane is *intelligent and amiable.*" "He was a *great but erring* man." "Religion *purifies and elevates* the mind." "He acted *vigorously and judiciously.*" "*Reason, passion* answer one great aim."

1. When one Adjective seems to modify the other, as in the following examples, no Comma is inserted between them; as, "a *dark yellow colour,*" "a *red hot* poker."

341. **Three or more words** of the same class, with or without a Conjunction, **must be separated by Commas**;

and the **last word**, if a **Noun** in the **Nominative Case**, should also be separated from the Verb by a **Comma**; as,

"*Poetry*, *music*, *and painting*, are fine arts." "David was a *brave*, *wise*, and *pious* prince." "Happy is the man who *honours*, *obeys*, *loves*, and *serves* his Creator." "You should seek knowledge *steadily*, *patiently*, and *perseveringly*."

342. When words **follow in pairs**, a **Comma** should be inserted **between each pair**; as,

"Truth is *fair and artless*, *simple and sincere*, *uniform and consistent*." "Whether we *eat or drink*, *labour or sleep*, we should be moderate."

343. **Simple members** of sentences **connected by comparatives** (*than*, *as*), are **separated** by a Comma, unless when the sentence is short; as,

"Better is a dinner of herbs with love, *than* a stalled ox and hatred with it." "*As* the hart panteth after the water-brooks, *so* doth my soul after Thee." "How much better it is to get wisdom *than* gold."

344. Words or phrases placed **in contrast with each other**, should be **separated** by a Comma; as,

"They are sometimes in *union with*, and sometimes in *opposition to*, the views of each other." "Though *deep*, yet *clear*; though *gentle*, yet not *dull*."

345. The **words or observations of another person** repeated, but not formally introduced as a quotation, should be **separated** from the context by a **Comma**; as,

"Plutarch calls lying, *the vice of slaves*."

346. When a **Conjunction is separated by a phrase or clause** from the second of the two sentences which it connects, such intervening phrase or clause should have a Comma placed before and after it; as,

"They set out early, *and*, *before the close of the day*, arrived at the destined place."

347. When a **Verb is understood in the clauses of a compound sentence**, a Comma is put in its stead; as,

"*Reading* makes a full man; conversation, a ready man; and writing, an exact man."

348. A word or phrase emphatically repeated should be **pointed off** by the Comma; as,

"Few, *few*, shall part where many meet."

349. The **SEMICOLON** is used for dividing a compound sentence into two or more parts, less closely connected than those which are separated by Commas.

350. When a sentence consists of **two** or **more members**, each constituting a **distinct proposition**, they are usually separated by the Semicolon; as,

"Perform your duty faithfully; for this will procure you the blessing of heaven." "Straws swim upon the surface; but pearls lie at the bottom." "Stones grow; vegetables grow and live; animals grow, live, and feel."

351. The **COLON** is used to divide a sentence into two or more parts, less connected than those which are separated by a Semicolon, but not so independent as to require a Period or Full Stop.

352. When a member of a sentence so **complete in itself** that a Period or Full stop might be used, is followed by another containing some additional observation, **a Colon should be inserted** between them; as,

"Study to acquire a habit of thinking: no study is more important."

353. When a sentence consisting of several members which are separated from each other by Semicolons, has its **sense suspended till the last clause**, that clause should be **separated from the others by a Colon**; as,

"If he has not been unfaithful to his king; if he has not proved a traitor to his country; if he has never given cause for such charges as have been preferred against him: why then is he afraid to confront his enemies?"

354. When an **example**, a **quotation**, or a **speech** is **formally introduced**, a **Colon** is usually inserted before it; and, by some writers, a *Dash*, in addition to the Colon; as,

"All our conduct towards men should be influenced by *this precept*: 'Do unto others as you would that others should do unto you.'" "The Arabians have a proverb which runs thus:—'Examine what is *said*, and not *him* who speaks.'"

1. But when an example or a quotation is introduced by the word '**as**,' a Semicolon should be placed before '**as**' and a Comma after it.

355. When a **sentence is complete** both in construction and sense, a **PERIOD** should be used.

The Period is also used to denote **abbreviation**, as in **Christian names**; *e.g.*, T. K. Wilson; or in **titles**; as, W. B. Carpenter, Esq., M.D., LL.D., C.B., F.R.S.

356. The **DASH** is used to denote an abrupt turn in a sentence, or where a significant or long pause is required; as,

"His children—but here my heart began to bleed—and I was forced to go on with another part of the portrait."

357. The **NOTE OF INTERROGATION** is put at the end of a sentence in which a question is **directly asked**, or **directly quoted**; as,

"What shall I do?" "Where shall I go?" "The Cyprians said to me, 'Why do you weep?'"

358. The **NOTE OF EXCLAMATION** is used after expressions of sudden emotion, and also after solemn or emphatic invocations or addresses; as,

"Eternity! thou pleasing, dreadful thought."

359. The **PARENTHESIS** is used to enclose, in the body of a sentence, some useful or explanatory observation which may be omitted, without affecting the sense, or injuring the grammatical construction; as,

"Know then this truth (enough for man to know),
Virtue alone is happiness below."

360. The **QUOTATION MARKS** are used only when **the actual words** of a writer or speaker are given.